professor • leader • mother • nurse • graduate • volunteer
artist • gofer • geologist
teacher • uncle • inte

therapist • young adult • athlete • designer • matriarch • prisoner • firefighter • executive • guard
coach • warden • inspector • rabbi • financier • brother • psychologist • handyman • custodian
ceo • conductor • scientist • bishop • comedian • cashier • journalist • dancer • techie

judge • elder • manager • cousin • counselor • doctor • pastor • grandmother • psychiatrist • refugee
father • cleric • stage manager • caregiver • tailor • actor • parent • mathematician
student • psychic • president • paramedic • aunt • cantor • architect • florist

# Simply Coaching

## for Your Highest and Best

To your Highest & Best! Lynn

**Lynn McIntyre Coffey**
MBA, MCC

Highest and Best Publishing, Inc.

futurist • grandfather • masseuse • politician • phlebotomist •
child • principal • police officer • agent • sister • adult • teacher •
mentor • teenager • administrator • miner • lawyer • social worker •

*Simply Coaching for Your Highest and Best*
Lynn McIntyre Coffey


Highest and Best Publishing, Inc.

Original materials presented first appeared in
*Simply Coaching: Ideas, Strategies, Methodologies, and Philosophies About Coaching for Coaches*, audiobook, ©1997.

*Note:* The examples within are about real people, real situations, real challenges, but with different names and places to keep their personal information private.



Cover, Interior design and eBook conversion: Rebecca Finkel, F + P Graphic Design

Library of Congress Catalog Number: 2018903107
BOOK CATEGORIES: Self-Discovery, Motivational & Inspirational, Coaching

ISBN print: 978-0-9998199-0-6
ISBN ebook: 978-0-9998199-2-0
ISBN audiobook: 978-0-9998199-1-3

Printed in the USA

*Christopher* and *Michael*
You live amazing lives.

*John*
You champion the best in me.

*You*
As you champion the Highest and Best
in yourself and others.

# Contents


Foreword Patrick Williams, EdD, MCC ........ vi

Introduction Why *Simply Coaching*, Why Now? ........ 1

Chapter 1 Your Highest and Best ........ 13

Chapter 2 The Powerful Four: Focus, Skills, Attitudes, Habits—A Mental Organizing Tool ........ 23

- Focus ........ 25
- Skills ........ 34
- Attitudes ........ 40
- Habits ........ 45

Chapter 3 Listen, Mirror, Path, Floodlight Method—The Anatomy of a Coaching Conversation ... 53

- Listen ........ 56
- Mirror ........ 61
- Path ........ 68
- Floodlight ........ 74

Chapter 4 Combining Techniques: Coaching Conversation and The Powerful Four .......... 81
Chapter 5 Your Standards and Boundaries .................. 91
Chapter 6 Creating a Full and Fulfilling Life ............. 109
Chapter 7 Clarity ............................................ 113
Chapter 8 Space Requirements ............................ 125
Time ............................................ 127
Physical ........................................ 131
Mental .......................................... 139
Emotional ...................................... 142
Spiritual ........................................ 146
Chapter 9 Personal Development ........................... 149
Afterword ................................................... 153
In Gratitude ................................................. 156
About Lynn ................................................... 158
Index .......................................................... 159
Pass Along Copy ............................................. 165

# Foreword

I am honored to write about the significant history and influence of *Simply Coaching*. As a founding member of the International Coach Federation in 1995 and a veteran coach, I came to know of Lynn's work very early on in the coaching movement. Notably, it influenced other early coaches and me and was referenced by those charged with identifying and defining what today is called the Core Competencies of the Coaching Profession.

Coaching evolved from many disciplines such as psychology, adult learning, management, and change theory. It sought to achieve elegance and simplicity that made it acceptable, accessible and useful to professionals and those who could benefit from coaching in all of its forms and niches. *Simply Coaching* struck me as the great representative of that.

Published in 1997 in audiobook form, *Simply Coaching* became a foundational piece of coaching curriculums and training programs including my own Institute for Life Coach Training. Lynn always encouraged adaptation of her work. She designed it to be flexible and open to the style and emphasis of individuals and professionals. In fact, my Big Five Coaching Method presented in my second book, *Becoming a Professional Life Coach,* and taught at the ILCT, is an adaptation of Lynn's work.

Lynn and I have stayed friends over the years. She remained a quiet influence to those who knew of her and resonated with her work ... just like many creatives.

Now, on *Simply Coaching*'s 20th anniversary, she is coming out—out to today's world of widespread coaching, training, niches, certifications, research and global reach. Her *Simply Coaching* is a treatise on coaching that is even more relevant and useful today to the practitioner and to those who benefit from the power of coaching conversations to achieve new insights, create intentions, and make desired changes in their lives.

**Patrick Williams,** EdD, MCC
Windsor, Colorado

psychiatrist • refugee • mentor • teenager • administrator • miner • lawy

INTRODUCTION

# Why *Simply Coaching*, Why Now?

*The purpose of coaching is to help individuals or groups be their Highest and Best.*

*In 1997 I did the unthinkable.* I sent my first book out into the world, *without me.* I did so with the understanding that if my work was worthwhile, it would have a life of its own, and if so, I was to return to it once my sons were raised.

Turns out, *Simply Coaching* has had quite a life. Without fanfare or obvious notoriety, it traveled around the world, teaching and influencing thought and development of the burgeoning profession of personal and professional coaching. Labeled timeless, it became a guide to establishing the coaching industry's core competencies and influenced methodologies, standards, ethics, and educational programs worldwide. Not bad for an orphan!

The time is right for *Simply Coaching* to return. Framed within the context of striving for our Highest and Best, this expanded work is for those who would like to learn our basic, but oh-so-powerful, coaching principles. Within, you will find help in personal insight and understanding, interpersonal communications skills, and finding and pursuing your direction. These are the very principles that we, as coaches, employ to help our clients reach their Highest and Best in a manner that is kind and respectful to themselves and others. In short, you will be aided in your pursuit of your Highest and Best as you create your life each moment of each day.

**You will be aided in your pursuit of your Highest and Best as you create your life each moment of each day.**

To say that throughout the world clashes of opinions and ideologies in politics, religions, nations, races, and classes are proving quite difficult for us would be an understatement. These conflicts are interfering with our ability to communicate and cooperate with one another at our best. And you and I both know that's a recipe for trouble!

We could all be part of the solution by improving the way we interact with one another. You see it all around you: the need to talk with one another in meaningful and respectful ways, the need to support one another to be our best, and the need to address the difficult issues at hand. Whether it's personal, professional, or societal, these interactions could be accomplished in thought-provoking and action-oriented ways that support who we are at our very Highest and Best, rather than our lowest and worst. Having coaching skills at your disposal can definitely help.

**We could all be part of the solution by improving the way we interact with one another.**

Imagine what your Highest and Best would be like if you were able to have meaningful and respectful conversations about the things most important to you. What if you had support to identify and take positive and productive actions toward your Highest and Best? If you are like most of us, you would love that! You would love the peace of mind knowing that you're on the right track, with agreed upon, doable actions and steps to guide you to your Highest and Best, be it for a major life event or simple everyday challenges. Wouldn't you love to be able to provide that for others as well?

How differently would you see yourself if you knew your individual improvements in understanding and interacting with yourself and others, and the authenticity of your life and your contributions had a direct impact on reversing the ever-increasing discord we are experiencing throughout the world? Wouldn't that be something?!

At its core, coaching helps individuals and groups be their Highest and Best. To be your Highest and Best, you need to know yourself more intimately than you may have previously experienced. Coaching leads to more profound self-knowledge, greater self-acceptance, and increased self-responsibility. As a result, you will find yourself strengthening, regaining, or perhaps most notably for some, experiencing personal power for the very first time.

Coaching happens in meaningful conversations, gently bringing light on difficult subjects, supporting self-discovery, championing visions, celebrating gifts, and illuminating next steps. These are the kinds of conversations we all hope, even desire, to have. The focusing tools of coaching foster understanding, agreement, and action. These three, when working in collaboration, help you and those you love, live, work and play with, adjust and thrive in our increasingly complicated world.

**Coaching happens in meaningful conversations.**

*Simply Coaching* provides a guide and tools for these conversations, simple or complicated, while accepting and championing one another with grace and dignity. During these discussions we identify what we need to do to be our Highest and Best, be it our focus, skills, attitudes, and habits, or how we manage our gifts, spaces, and development.

As you develop your coaching skills, you will discover that your conversations become much more useful because you are incorporating many of the gifts I identified early on in my practice.

I assure you that if you enter into conversations with the following in mind, you will be far more successful and satisfied with the results:

- Seeing without judgment;
- Understanding with insight and discernment;
- Simplifying, saying things in a manner that is easily understood;
- Creating new awareness and understanding;
- Guiding and advising without attachment to the outcome; and,
- Creating with clarity, vision, and insight.

Just as each coach has a variety of capabilities and gifts to draw upon, so do you. The more skilled and comfortable you are with your talents, the more easily you will employ them, according to what is needed in the coaching moment. All gifts seek expression. Some gifts you are born with, some gifts are developed. Most gifts can be learned and all gifts can be improved. Making the most of your gifts will help you reach your Highest and Best in coaching as well as in creating a full and fulfilling life.

**All gifts seek expression.**

In 1988, determined to understand how I kept getting such amazing results with my consulting clients, I drew the following diagram to illustrate many of the different roles and gifts I drew upon when engaged with my clients.

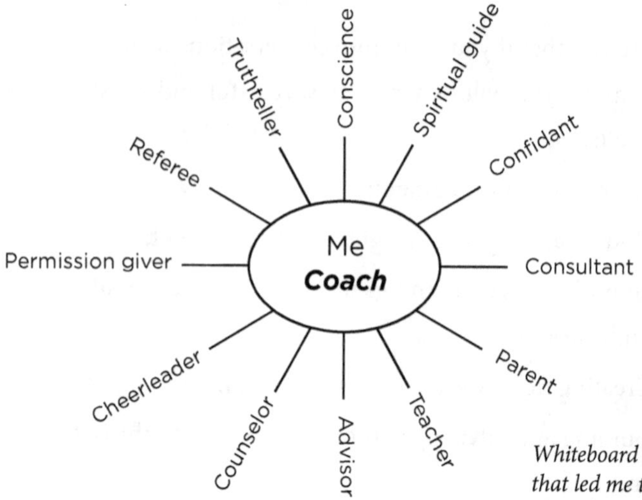


*Whiteboard session that led me to the idea of coaching.*

It was this exercise that originally led me to realize that what I did and who I was becoming was very similar to my brothers' high school athletic coaches. Without realizing the significance, I began calling myself a coach. I set to work creating, developing, and enhancing the ideas, methods, tools, skills, and standards and boundaries for my work as a coach. This work ultimately influenced and helped define a new industry.

At the same time I was developing my version of coaching; others were also looking at their constellation of gifts and giving them the name of "coaching" as well. This resulted in the development of a diversity of styles, methods, and approaches to coaching. This was and is a very good thing, as there is a tremendous variety among those who want and need coaching.

You have your own style as well. You will adopt the methods and tools that fit your background, personality, and gifts. And please, don't let anyone tell you that there is only one way to coach or that you can only ask "meaningful" questions! These are styles that some have taken on and insisted upon but are certainly not the only way to coach!

**And please, don't let anyone tell you that there is only one way to coach or that you can only ask "meaningful" questions!**

Now, let's get to you. Take a minute and grab a journal or notebook; you are going to want one as you continue to read and work through this book.

It's your turn to create a circle of your capabilities and gifts. What do you bring to the table? You might be surprised by how many you have or you might be at a loss to think of any. Don't worry; they're in there. Just start with what you can think of for now. Look back at mine to get some ideas. As you continue to read this book, do keep your journal handy. Add to your circle as new ideas come to mind. You'll have many opportunities to think more specifically about your amazing gifts. I promise!

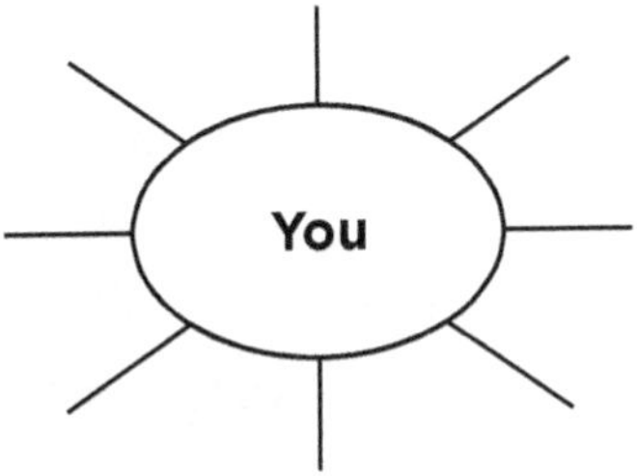

As you continue reading, see yourself in the role of coach, not necessarily as a professional, but as an approach you take. Imagine how you might use the ideas presented when talking or working with someone—family, friend, client, colleague, or subordinate, even your boss! By blending these powerful ideas, skills, and methodologies with your own strengths and knowledge, you will improve your ability to have focused, meaningful conversations. Not only that, you will understand what it takes to be your Highest and Best and how to guide and be guided on this amazing journey. You will be in a much better position to create your reality based on your dreams and desires for Highest and Best.

We are not living in easy times. There is a daily barrage of lowest and worst trying to take us down. My hope for you is that you can use these tools for conversations, personal insights, standards and boundaries, clarity, space, and personal development to coach yourself and others to a better life. Doing so will make life better for you and those around you and will contribute to making our world a better place.

Just one word of caution: when coaching another person, your job is not to fix them or to get attached to their result—that is the job of each individual. If you are using these tools to coach yourself (yes, you can do that too!), getting attached to your own results may be a bit trickier.

**When coaching another person, your job is not to fix them or to get attached to their result—that is the job of each individual.**

Bottom line: these tools are designed to help you be a support to yourself and others while striving for Highest and Best. Plain and simple.

Now let's take a look at what we are going to cover.

## Your Basic Tools

It is important for you to have the best choice of methods, tools, skills, and understandings to guide and support you in this marvelous dance called coaching. If you are a professional coach, you have undoubtedly seen elements of these ideas throughout the coaching industry. If you are new to coaching as a profession, looking to add to your skill set, or looking for ways to grow, hold on tight because we are going to cover a lot of ground quickly.

**It is important for you to have the best choice of methods, tools, skills, and understandings to guide and support you in this marvelous dance called coaching.**

## Your Highest and Best

Understanding and adopting a Highest and Best approach will make your world brighter, happier, and healthier. It will contribute to more productive and satisfying relationships, work, love, and play. Sometimes, you just need to be pointed in the right direction. In Chapter 1 we will look at what Highest and Best means and what it doesn't and ways to point you in the right direction.

### The Powerful Four:

Focus, Skills, Attitudes & Habits Method

As a mental organizing tool for coaching, *The Powerful Four* Method will help you gain a better understanding of yourself and others, specifically and in general. It provides a simple yet powerful structure to assist you in identifying the specific elements as well as actions needed for success. All things being equal, if these four things are in place, you can't help but succeed.

### The Basic Coaching Conversation:

Listen, Mirror, Path, Floodlight Method

If you are like most of us, you crave to be heard and understood. You seek an understanding of who you are as an individual. You search for focus, direction, meaning, and purpose. You want to know where you are going and what to do next. Straightforward and elegant, the Listen, Mirror, Path, Floodlight Method in Chapter 3 will guide you through the steps of a successful coaching conversation to accomplish these goals.

### Combining Methods

In Chapter 4, *The Coaching Conversation and the Powerful Four* are combined into a simple format, creating an incredibly dynamic and powerful tool. Presented in outline form, it can be used as a roadmap as you practice and develop your coaching skills.

## Standards and Boundaries

Over the years, it became abundantly clear to me that a good working knowledge of standards and boundaries is vital to a healthy approach to coaching, not to mention your own personal and professional life. I believe you'll find that when you are clear about your standards and have appropriate boundaries to protect them, life gets smoother and you have a much better chance being the kind of person you want to be at your Highest and Best.

## Creating a Full and Fulfilling Life

More and more of us have come to understand that we create our realities. Fundamental to creating a full and fulfilling life requires that you foster clarity, have enough space—time, physical, mental, emotional, and spiritual—and tend to your personal development.

We are at the forefront of our next level of consciousness, to a higher way of being, where we are aware that we create our reality and we actively and consciously participate in its creation. The material presented in *Simply Coaching* will give you the basic tools to guide your creations as you intentionally create through the power of your thoughts, words, and actions in a manner reflecting your Highest and Best.

**We are at the forefront of our next level of consciousness, to a higher way of being, where we are aware that we create our reality and we actively and consciously participate in its creation.**

By applying what's contained within *Simply Coaching*, you will find that your relationships become easier, your challenges not as difficult, and your day-to-day life just a lot nicer.

Over the years, these simple processes and ideas have been successfully used by myself and many others to help countless thousands of individuals, groups, and organizations. The results have been significant, quick, effective, and sustainable.

I invite you to join me and rise to the challenge of being your Highest and Best!

Now, let's get to work!

CHAPTER 1

# Your Highest and Best

*On behalf of the majority of the world,*
*I can state with great confidence*
*that we would prefer you*
*to strive for your Highest and Best.*

*Highest and Best* is a mindset, a way of life. It is not a destination. It comes from looking for and supporting the best in yourself and others. It may sound like a pretty lofty concept until you realize how accessible it is to you and the power it has in supporting you in creating a much better life for yourself and those for whom you care.

Focusing on your Highest and Best affords you a fantastic view of your life, gently supporting the "all too human" aspiration to be far more than you are now. Neglecting it gives rise to mediocrity at best and downright destruction at worst! That is not what you are going for, is it?

Becoming your Highest and Best results from an alignment between what you value, what is important to you, and your thoughts, words, and deeds. You are authentic, true to yourself. It is reflected in the reality you create, your relationship with yourself and others, and the experiences you have, day in and day out, throughout your lifetime.

**Highest and Best results from an alignment between what you value, what is important to you, and your thoughts, words, and deeds.**

Highest and Best shows up in predictable ways: acceptance, non-judgmental, support, empathy, genuine concern for others, positive self-image, hope, inspiration, truth, honesty, success, generosity, and integrity.

Lowest and worst also shows up in predictable ways: critical, rejection, judgment, blaming, ridicule, isolation, lack of sympathy or genuine concern for others, lying, stealing, cheating, and failure.

Your Highest and Best isn't about being perfect, that is not possible in this reality. Nor is it about setting unrealistic expectations of yourself, others, or life. To me, it means focusing on what is important to me and being the best I can be in the moment, over and over and over again, whatever my focus, whatever experiences I may encounter on my journey. It also means looking for and supporting the best in myself, others, and in situations.

**Your Highest and Best isn't about being perfect, that is not possible in this reality.**

The concept of Highest and Best is also very powerful in your interpersonal and coaching relationships. Many a client, individual, and group reached far greater heights when their Highest and Best was identified and championed by their coach, parent, partner, or boss. Making a habit of seeing yourself and others at their Highest and Best has the potential of changing your relationships and your experience of the world. It provides opportunities to support that which is good in you, others, and the world.

**Making a habit of seeing yourself and others at their Highest and Best has the potential of changing your relationships and your experience of the world.**

During initial intake meetings, a savvy college entrance coach asks parents to "sing the praise of their child." One mother, whose son's negative moods caused her great concern, noticed that as she spoke of her son's qualities, his confidence shifted, his body straightened, his chin came up, and his eyes became engaged. It was then that she realized that his sour mood was in large part fueled by the way she was seeing him, always looking for any imperfections she should correct. She committed to change this and to see him at his Highest and Best on a regular basis. This resulted in astonishing changes in her son's demeanor and confidence and, not surprisingly, their relationship.

Using a Highest and Best approach will help you embrace your possibilities and those of others. If you're wondering how you were doing, begin by listening to your own thoughts. Are they supportive or critical? Listen to what you say and how you talk about things. Watch what you do. Are you leading yourself to your Highest and Best or your lowest and worst? Your own introspection will pay off, giving you a clear picture of yourself and how you are treating others. Observing it in others will provide you with insight into who they are and where they are headed. When this is done in a non-judgemental way, you will have a much better chance of seeing *your* Highest and Best, and *theirs*.

Let's look at how focusing on Highest and Best might play out for something specific.

Stan values his car. What might Stan's Highest and Best be when it comes to his owning a car? Keeping it gassed, serviced, cleaned, repaired, and insured would be a reasonable, achievable start for Stan. For Bill, aiming for that might be completely overwhelming at first; gas and insurance may be his best for now. In time, Bill's focus on his best will make it easier for him to find a way to include servicing and repair.

Judy didn't practice Highest and Best. She practiced a get-by approach to owning a car. It was easy for her to keep her car gassed and insured and that was as far as she went. She ignored the dashboard light indicating it was time to service her car.

Months went by and the check engine light illuminated. She ignored this light as well. Within a very short time, the engine of her little car was destroyed. It had run out of oil. It was a tough lesson for her. From that point on, Judy understood that being her lowest and worst had significant and costly consequences.

With this thought in mind, you might ask yourself: "What can I reasonably do that would get me to my Highest and Best as it relates to my car?" Perhaps a habit of filling your gas tank when it gets to the quarter-full mark, or, changing the oil on a regular basis; maybe some gratitude thrown in for the fact that you have a car (if you do!) and the resources to keep it up, maybe even a special weekend washing.

How you think about something, what you say about it and what you do with it, will all reflect how you value it and the experience you have with it. The same is true for people and experiences. If you're wondering how you are doing, just look at your results. If things aren't the way you would like them to be, listen to your own thoughts. Are they supportive or critical? Listen to what you talk about and what you say. Watch what you do. You might find you are excellent at supporting yourself and others or you might find that you repeatedly shoot yourself in the foot with thoughts, words, and deeds that drag you and others down. Or you may realize that you support others thoughts, words, and deeds more than you support your own. The important thing is to know yourself and to be able to make the adjustments needed to be your best.

Now it's your turn. Get your journal out and do a little writing on these questions. Do it a few times to get the hang of it.

- Pick something you value: person, place, thing, idea, or experience.
- With this in mind, what thoughts, words, and deeds would support you in achieving your Highest and Best?
- Given the internal and external resources you have available, what is reasonable to ask of yourself?
- Set daily, weekly and monthly goals for yourself.
- Tell others about your goals.
- Now that you know what you are aiming for, focus on doing your best each day.
- Be honest with yourself about how well you are meeting your goals.
- Hold yourself accountable.
  - Check in with yourself daily:
    - How am I doing?
    - How well am I meeting my goals?

- Am I doing what I said I was going to do?
- Am I doing something that makes it hard for me to keep my promises to myself?
- Is something or someone in my way?
- Adjust as needed.

- Ask someone you trust and respect to give you feedback about how well you are doing and how honest you are being with yourself.

Sometimes we set goals that are too high or too low. We might expect results with little or no effort or in too short of a period of time. Again, be honest with yourself. It's important. And don't beat yourself up when you don't meet your goals, that won't help. Be kind to yourself and encourage yourself to continue.

Here is a very important part of this whole approach. Sometimes your Highest and Best will look magnificent and other times it won't. Even when you are at your lowest, the attributes in the Highest and Best approach can be of great service.

**Sometimes your Highest and Best will look magnificent and other times it won't.**

Years after I wrote the original *Simply Coaching*, an illness left me in a very dark and arduous place. Stripped of vitality, I was literally at my lowest and worst. Harnessing the power of Highest and Best came to my rescue in a big way.

I established three daily rules that I believed would point me in the right direction.

- Do the best I can in the moment.
- Create some order each day.
- Celebrate at least one victory each day.

At this particular point in my journey, my Highest and Best wasn't very high nor anywhere near my best. Some days, my victory was as simple as making my bed, and others, a better attitude, a sparkle of hope.

It worked. Over time, my formula for shooting for my Highest and Best in the moment helped me navigate my way out of that dark period to a much better place. It has become a mantra for me when life gets tough. I cannot tell you how many times I have turned to this simple practice to redirect myself to a better place.

Feel free to use any or all parts of my formula to make it your own! Think of it as bread crumbs, leading you back to your Highest and Best. Remember, we need you, me, everyone, to be our Highest and Best as often and for as long as we can. It is important.

## The Power of Permission

Early in my coaching career, I learned the power of permission. I experienced client after client who, upon receiving outside permission (in these cases from me), was able to take on new challenges, handle difficult jobs, escape abusive relationships, change jobs, start businesses, return to school, all soaring to success and their Highest and Best. At first, I wondered, "Who am I to give them permission?" It didn't take long to realize it wasn't me so much as it was someone believing in them and them hearing what they longed to hear: "You can do it! You can be your Highest and Best!"

There were times that many of them also needed permission to quit. I have lost count of the number of people, frustrated and scared, who wanted to throw in the towel as they were striving to accomplish their goals. They all found amazing strength to carry on when they knew they had permission to quit. I have seen it with clients, friends, and family, even myself. I can't think of one person I have worked with whom I "gave permission to quit," who actually gave up on their dreams. It was as if knowing that they could quit gave them the strength and courage to hang in there until they met with success.

You have my permission to take on your greatest dreams and succeed. If the going gets too tough, you also have my permission to quit. Keeping your Highest and Best in your sights will guide you, moment-by-moment, day-to-day, in your work, play and relationships. Like I said before, some days, your Highest and Best will look amazing and sometimes it won't. Embracing this can be a great motivator and increase your compassion for yourself and others. This can be life-changing, particularly if you are like the many who have more compassion for others than for themselves.

**Keeping your Highest and Best in your sights will guide you, moment-by-moment, day-to-day, in your work, play and relationships.**

As you get to know yourself from the vantage point of Highest and Best, you may find it necessary to make changes and adjustments to your thoughts, words, and deeds to point yourself in the right direction. Don't be afraid to get some support if you find you are continually running yourself or others down or just can't seem to do what it takes to be your best. Some of these habits can be hard to break, but it's so worth it.

Now let me show you some tools that will make aiming for your Highest and Best a bit easier.

CHAPTER 2

# The Powerful Four: Focus, Skills, Attitudes, Habits

*A Mental Organizing Tool*

*I would like* to introduce you to the first tool I developed when I started coaching. I needed something to keep myself mentally organized and on track as I worked with my clients. When I began my coaching practice, the only coaching model I was aware of was in athletics. So I asked myself, "What does the athletic coach do to help their athletes achieve their best?" I determined that there were four powerful emphases: focus, skills, attitudes, and habits.

Coaches help their athletes focus on what they are trying to accomplish, from the big picture to the detail. Focus is fundamental to the athlete's ability to perform and excel. Therefore, it is always checked, always nurtured. Often when there is a problem with an athlete's performance, it can be traced back to focus.

The coach has a keen understanding of the skills their athletes need to perform. They continually evaluate their skill levels, developing new skills, as well as enhancing existing ones.

The success of many an athlete hinges upon the attitudes, beliefs, and convictions that affect the way they see the world. The coach monitors, adjusts, and develops their athletes' attitudes, to support success in their sport, as well as in their lives.

Good habits are the day-to-day disciplines that embody the focus, skills, and attitudes necessary for success. The athletic coach identifies the essential habits for their athletes' success and helps them establish and maintain them. The coach also works to weed out habits that are counterproductive to the athlete's best interest.

It quickly became apparent to me that these powerful four would be an excellent mental organizing tool to understand what my clients needed to be successful and in helping me see what was holding them back. They have become fundamental in creating powerful shifts, changes, and growth.

Let's go through each of these and apply them to you and how to use them in your coaching conversations.

## Focus

Your focus is where you're looking, where you're headed; it's where you put your energy. Ideally, your focus is clear, strong, steady, and flexible. It moves smoothly from the big picture to detail and points in between. When your focus is strong, you can identify it; you know why you have it, and you can maintain it. It is appropriate for your vision and goals. You easily manage to blend compatible focuses, effortlessly moving between them. You are comfortable working in each level of detail, directing your attention as needed.

**Focus is where you're looking, where you're headed.**

When your focus doesn't support your success, it is inappropriate, muddy, weak, wobbly, inflexible, or stuck in the detail or the big picture. You are fragmented, disorganized, and unable to accomplish much. You might move from idea to idea, project to project without the satisfaction of seeing anything to completion.

You will find all sorts of combinations of focus problems: chaotic focus, lack of focus, wrong focus and moving focus are just a few. Understanding and correcting focusing problems is the first order of business.

### *Chaotic Focus*

Dana was frantic. She was losing her business. Her one-time successful physical therapy business was in a downward spiral, and she was at a loss as to how to turn it around. Referral sources were reluctant to send her patients. Her employees were acting out. She was in crippling debt, and her banker had lost hope that she would recover. If things didn't change fast, Dana would have to close the doors. She needed help and fast.

During our initial conversation, Dana darted from staff to finances, to services, to marketing, to referral agencies, back to staff, off to finances, and looping around again to marketing. After a while, I said to her, "I bet your desk is a mess." She looked at me with surprise, "How did you know that?" "Well," I answered, "by the way you're talking. Your thinking is chaotic. It lacks focus. There isn't a sense of order or priorities that would allow you to have a neat and orderly desk." Her business was failing in part because her focus was chaotic.

We needed to get Dana working on her camera lens. She needed to be able to focus if she was ever going to see her way clear of disaster. My plan was to get her to focus on her immediate surroundings and then move her focus to her thinking. Once that was in place, we could move into her organization. We started with her desk. Her first assignment was to clean it up, get it in order, and keep it that way. No more desk chaos. Because she was in the habit of leaving things out so she wouldn't forget them, she was to make a list of all the things that needed her attention as she put things away.

Then we moved to her thinking. We began to organize her mind using an easy and efficient time management system that enabled her to identify her priorities, keep on top of her projects, and put away and retrieve working materials as needed. It worked. Her focus began to sharpen. Skills and habits essential to her success were coming into play. And the most exciting improvement was her change of attitude. She was willing to do whatever it took to save her business. She allowed herself to grow first, correcting her focusing issues, before we moved into her organization. You'll hear more about Dana later.

### *Moving Focus*

Burt had no idea that he had trouble maintaining his focus. With years of experience in home rental management, Burt knew he could build his own successful agency if he could just get it off the ground. He just needed a little professional coaching. His first assignment was to create an overview of his business and then fill in the details. He returned to his next session empty-handed but very excited to tell me about a new real estate investment program he was going to represent. It was exhilarating to him, creating a network of individuals to invest in an out-of-state land development. He explained in great detail how his potential success with property investing would be a great way for him to support his home rental management start-up.

The next time I saw Burt, he was a bit down in the dumps. He wasn't sure the real estate investment program would work. However, he did have a new idea on which to focus. He would flip houses to make enough money to start his management agency.

It was apparent that Burt was unable to maintain his focus. He was caught up in what I call "the entrepreneurial field of rabbits"—chasing any opportunity no matter what it was, good or flakey. It took his focus off his goals. If Burt had any chance of successfully developing his home rental management business, his ability to stay focused had to improve.

**"The entrepreneurial field of rabbits"—chasing any opportunity no matter what it was.**

Burt immediately understood the concept of the "entrepreneurial field of rabbits." We agreed to be on the lookout for rabbits. As soon as we saw one, we pointed him right back to his goal. At first, I did most of the seeing. Eventually, he got the hang of it. We also began seeing a pattern in his behavior. As soon as he hit a roadblock, he wanted to shift course. Burt needed support in dealing with roadblocks. It became an important part of our coaching sessions. Burt learned a valuable lesson about maintaining his focus and knowing when and why he was getting distracted. Burt uses the image of "chasing rabbits" when something pops up that could distract him from focusing on his successful home rental management business.

### *Wrong Focus*

The wrong focus can create some serious mistakes. Jim, an East Coast furniture manufacturer, wanted to sell his business. It consumed his thinking. It was a perfectly good business that he enjoyed running. He'd had it for a while, and it was successful, but he explained to me in great detail all the reasons why selling it would be the right thing to do.

**The wrong focus can create some serious mistakes.**

None of Jim's reasons made sense to me, indicating that I needed to find out what he wasn't talking about. I poked around different areas of his life, looking for the real problem. When I asked him how his wife felt about the business, his demeanor changed, his head dropped, and he started mumbling, my clue to dig deeper. As I listened, it became evident that his focus on getting rid of his business was, in fact, a red herring. By making his business the problem, he didn't have to focus on his personal life. As it turned out, his marriage was in trouble.

Jim needed emotional support to help him move his focus to his real challenge–his marriage. He accepted a referral to a marriage and family counselor knowing that I would support him through the therapeutic process. It was important that he be able to move his focus between his business and his marriage. Ultimately, Jim didn't give up his business. Unfortunately, his marriage did end. And as tragic as that was, it would have been a greater tragedy for Jim to have both lost his marriage and thrown his business away. He learned a valuable lesson about over-focusing on his business as a means of distraction and the potential devastating consequences of not taking care of the real problem.

*Big Picture/Detail*

We all have preferences in the way we like to look at things, how we like to focus: big picture or detail. Some can only stay in the big picture, others the detail. Others can move from big picture to detail or detail to big picture. It impacts the way we think and learn. Take some time to figure out which one you are. Knowing your preference can save you a lot of time and frustration.

**We all have preferences in the way we like to look at things, how we like to focus: big picture or detail.**

Cameron, a high school senior, was struggling with a statistics class. He explained to me that he was often confused during class, failing quizzes, but acing exams. He was lost until he understood all of the detail of the statistical models he was learning and that usually didn't happen until right before the exam. When I asked him how his teacher presented the materials, he described a big picture to detail presentation. Once he understood he was a detail to big picture person, Cameron accepted my advice to study the details of the statistical models before his teacher introduced them. It worked like a charm. He was no longer confused in class. He became an active participant, earning high marks.

Amy, another student, had a different type of problem. She understood the broad-brush, big picture approach her history professor took when explaining World War II. But when her teacher started to fill in the details of people, places, and events to support his lecture, Amy's mind began to swirl. To help manage her confusion, I suggested it might be helpful for her to create a timeline of the major events of the war. Using this overview, she filled in the details below each event. Now things began to make sense to her. She was able to see the big picture and the details all at one time.

Gary, an electronics engineer, wanted to start a business building computer components. Well equipped with knowledge about his product, his market, and his competition, he seemed all set to go. To be successful as an entrepreneur, Gary would have to be able to move between the big picture and detail. As we began working on his business plan, a focusing challenge emerged. He could talk about the big picture, but he loved the detail. He loved it to the point of distraction. After several months of trying to balance Gary's focus, we both came to the same conclusion: big picture thinking was extremely difficult for him, and he didn't like it nor did he want to do it. He realized that he would be much happier going back to work for someone else in a technical capacity where he could submerge himself in detail rather than fighting to constantly move between the big picture and detail required to operate his own business. He understood that to be satisfied in his work, he needed to align his focus with his preference.

Beverley left the Army equipped with just about everything she needed to become an entrepreneur. Unfortunately, during the 15 years she served as a Non-Commissioned Officer she had trained herself not to see the big picture so that she could focus exclusively on the details of her commander's plans. As a civilian, it took her a while to appreciate her natural talents and preference in big picture thinking. When she learned to rely on the gifts and talents of others to deal with the details of her plans, she was able to grow and thrive as a CEO.

Understanding, clarifying, and supporting focus is one of the primary jobs of a coach. It is also a primary function of success. To determine someone's focus, just listen to what they say. They will "tell you" quite clearly. If they jump around a lot, they have a focusing problem. This might be as a result of not having good skills, or it could be biochemical; you know, ADD type of biochemistry. They may be focusing on what they think they should vs. what they want. They might be asking themselves to focus in a way that is just not possible.

**Understanding, clarifying, and supporting focus is one of the primary jobs of a coach.**

First things first—get your focus in the right direction and support it through time management, conversations, check-ins, even asking yourself throughout the day: What am I focusing on and is it supporting me?

Answer the following questions in your journal:

- What is my focus?
- Does it support my overall goals?
- How well am I able to maintain my focus?
- What takes me off my focus?
- What helps me regain focus when it is lost?

All of this makes a lot of sense, doesn't it? Now, let's move forward to see how skills come into play.

## Skills

When working with focus, the skill requirements to achieve your goals begin to surface. When you have the skills you need to accomplish a task, you know what you need to do, in the order it needs to be done. You know what tools you need and if you need help. You also know that you can find the skills you need outside of yourself. Family and friends, employees and bosses, businesses and other professionals, even subcontractors are possible sources.

**When you have the skills you need to accomplish a task, you know what you need to do, in the order it needs to be done.**

When you lack the necessary skills to accomplish your goals, life can be pretty frustrating. You might be unaware of your missing skills. Or, you may believe you could never develop the skills necessary to accomplish your goals. It may not even dawn on you that someone else could provide the skills you need. You might be in denial, refusing to accept that you are missing a necessary skill or that it's even required. You go without and wonder why things don't work. Your efforts become lopsided, some parts of your personal or work life are taking off while other parts are stuck. Ultimately, your growth is impeded.

**When you lack the necessary skills to accomplish your goals, life can be pretty frustrating.**

You can help yourself and others with skill-obstacles by identifying the skills needed and finding ways to either develop the skills needed, sharpen them, or acquire them. This, in and of itself, can be an incredible gift.

So how do you know what skills are needed? Some are obvious, others aren't. You can often identify the skills necessary to meet specific goals through common sense. Other skills may not be as apparent. In this case, a fact-finding mission is needed. Library or online research, curriculum reviews, personal interviews with successful individuals who have similar goals or are in the field of interest can make understanding skill requirements come alive. Don't skip this step. Missing skills can seriously impede progress.

Once identified, the skills list will fall into three categories: "has" and "doesn't have" and points in between. Now is the time to revisit one's goals. Do you or the other person have enough skills to meet the targets? Is there enough capacity to acquire missing skills through learning or purchasing? Is there enough time, money? If the answers are yes, then proceed. If the answers are no, it may be necessary to go back to the drawing board.

Skill challenges show up in a variety of ways.

### *Missing Skills*

Harold, a very polished real estate executive, had created a great service for small businesses. By evaluating new and renewing office leases, he could find ways of saving businesses up to 25 percent of their annual rent while striking excellent deals for his clients. Upon meeting Harold, you would think that success would be rolling right in, but it wasn't. He couldn't figure out what was wrong; everything seemed to be in place. Well focused, he appeared to have all the skills he needed for his business: great product, great presentations, great selling ability, well-capitalized, well-connected, and well-organized. He just couldn't figure out why more potential customers weren't signing up for his services.

I asked Harold if he would be willing to do a role-playing exercise with me. I wanted him to sell me on his service. His presentation was flawless. He knew his facts and figures and all the reasons why I should sign up. He was phenomenal until it was time to transition from presentation to close, the point at which he should be asking me for my business. There it was, the missing skill. By examining each step of the selling process, we understood where he was stuck. He didn't know how to close the deal.

This lack of closing skills had been difficult to detect at first because some potential clients jumped at the chance to sign up for his services without being asked. Harold hadn't realized he had a problem. We worked on transition and closing skills until he was comfortable asking for the sale. With the help of "another set of eyes," Harold was able to see where his problem was, learn valuable closing skills, and went on to realize the success he knew he could have.

Collin, a bright, eager college student entered college with just about everything a student could need except for good study skills. Not surprising, he struggled academically until he found Jesse, an excellent tutor who taught him the powerful study skills she had learned in high school. With the right skills, Collin not only succeeded in his undergraduate program; he went on to become a very successful accountant. The skills he learned from Jesse made it possible for him to soar.

### *Not Applying Existing Skills*

Sarah was a president of a major insurance company and mother of three girls. Her responsibilities at the office were challenging and rewarding. She had quite a large staff, including a secretary, and a new assistant. She took advantage of all the appropriate seminars and educational programs her company offered.

Her life at home was another story. Within no time of returning home from work, Sarah's anxiety level would climb. She was completely overwhelmed by household and parenting responsibilities. While she kept hoping her girls would be able to help her with some of the chores, it never happened. Instead, she would argue with them, feeling more and more out of control. Then her husband would step in and ask what he could do to help. Frustrated and angry, Sarah would respond, "Nothing."

During her coaching sessions, I wanted Sarah to see how her success in one area of her life could be applied to another. We began by comparing and contrasting her work and home life. At work, she was clear about her responsibilities and those of her subordinates. She had employees to whom she could delegate, and she took advantage of educational opportunities.

At first Sarah assumed that her home life would take care of itself. When she admitted that things were not "taking care of themselves," she thought she would have to take an approach that was foreign to her. But when we looked at things at home from the perspective of her management style at work, a different picture emerged. At home, there were no assignments of responsibilities. Sarah just took everything on herself. She thought she had no one to delegate to. She was out of control with her girls and didn't know how to deal with them.

Using her success at work as a model, Sarah realized she needed to do four things:

- define home responsibilities
- assign specific jobs to everyone in the family
- hire a service to do the cleaning and laundry
- take a parenting class

Sarah just needed to apply the same organizational and management skills she used at work to her home. When she looked at her home situation through the eyes of what skills were needed, it moved from being emotional to being doable. Her home life went from miserable to happy!

### *Skills that are Unattainable*

Sometimes, no matter how hard we try, we just can't develop the skills we need to pursue a specific goal. Sophie dreamed of being a comedic stage actress. She was funny and had great stage presence. There was only one problem: Sophie had no aptitude for memorization. She tried several different techniques to help her, all to no avail. She was about to give up on the stage altogether when she learned about a local improvisation group. She auditioned and hit the jackpot. She found a way to perform that didn't require memorizing anything. Her quick wit propelled her to become a featured performer in a hilarious political improvisational group, touring the country to packed audiences.

### *Acquiring Skills*

There are many ways to acquire the skills needed to succeed. If you are coaching, you can encourage your clients to teach themselves, you can teach them, or you can refer them to other professionals. You can recommend books, classes, or training programs. If appropriate, you can also encourage them to buy the skills. You can apply the same recommendations to yourself!

**There are many ways to acquire the skills needed to succeed.**

When you are unable to acquire a necessary skill, you don't have to give up completely. You may need to find, as Sophie did, an alternative goal that encompasses many of the aspects of your original goal. Or, you may take a good look at the skills and talents you wanted to use and figure out where else you could use them and adapt your focus accordingly.

Write in your journal the answers to the following questions:

- What are my goals?
- What skills are required for me to be successful?
- How well have I developed these skills?
- How can I improve or get these skills?
- What can I do if I find I can't develop or obtain these skills?

## Attitudes

An attitude is a mental or emotional position from which you view the world, yourself, events, people, just about anything. It can encompass any number of vantage points: gratitude and appreciation,

**An attitude is a mental or emotional position from which yo view the world, yourself, events, people, just about anything.**

positive or negative responses, tenacity, victimhood, resentment, superiority or inferiority—the list goes on.

During my nephew's college graduation, I shared with him a powerful realization I had come to since I was in college about the people who were happy, prosperous, and fulfilled. They all seemed to have one thing in common: an attitude that supported them in achieving their desires.

When you have an attitude that supports you, you have great conviction. You accept that life will provide challenges. You accept victory as well as defeat. You are pleasant to be around and are accepting of others. You know who you are and what is and is not acceptable to you.

When you have an attitude that doesn't support you, you are often frustrated and angry. You may believe you are better than others or believe that most are better than you. You are unable to see opportunities for what they are, or you don't see them at all.

When you are aware of someone's attitude about something, you know his or her mental and emotional positions. You can understand how events, interactions, or circumstances can affect them. When you see them having trouble, you might need to help them change their attitude. The same is true for you!

### *Changing Attitudes*

It's not always easy to influence a change in attitude. To do so, there must be a change in the position from which things are viewed. This shift can happen as a result of many things, such as events, experiences, new information, education, and other people's influence. You can help create changes in attitudes by using your gifts, such as insight, permission, discernment, and language.

When I need to help someone see things differently, I use several different approaches. Sometimes I will tell a story. At other times, I will suggest that the person either figuratively or literally move to another spot for a minute to look at something from a different angle. Sometimes, that's all it takes. Other times they won't budge. And still other times, the person can move to the new position, but can't stay there without a lot of support.

Another approach is to create an internal motivation for change by asking and observing what a particular attitude is doing to your life. Watch for a short period, a week or two. Simply watch that attitude in action. When it comes up, notice what you're thinking about, look at the pictures in your mind, feel the emotions, and note the circumstances. After a week or two, you should have enough information to create a shift.

### *The Effects of Attitudes:* Good and Bad

Barbara was a marketing rep for a large healthcare organization. She was having trouble getting along at work. As we talked, I began picking up an attitude that caused her to believe that everyone should work as hard as she did. I asked her to observe her internal dialogue for a week.

The next day she went to work early, and no one else was there. She heard herself think, "Huh. I'm the only one here early. I'm the only one who cares." Martyrdom gets an early start. Her boss arrives and doesn't even notice her. The other reps arrive. They engage in morning chitchat and a few minutes of laughter with the boss. Then, it quiets down as everyone begins their day.

The little voice inside of her, motivated by her attitude, said, "The boss should like me better. I work harder." That fed a growing resentment toward the other reps. According to the voice in Barbara's head, they obviously weren't working as hard as she was. At lunchtime, she was alone. She just had to work through lunch to get her work done. Besides, none of her coworkers had invited her to have lunch with them. "No one likes me," she sulked. In reality, since she had declined their invitations so often, they just stopped asking. Barbara's response was to distance herself from them.

When we worked with her belief that she had to work so hard, we began to see that this one attitude and the thinking that went with it was causing her interpersonal problems at work. She began to understand the other reps reactions to her. She realized that as long as she held this belief, she would be very lonely in the workplace.

But how could she change her attitude? She believed she had to work long hours to do her job. As we talked, it became apparent that beneath this attitude were some missing skills. We looked at her work habits and realized they were not supporting her. We developed her skills in time and project management. It didn't take long for her to master these new skill-sets and create good work habits. As she accomplished more, she needed less time. She was coming in and leaving work with everyone else. She even had time to go to lunch. Her original attitude changed. As a result, many other things shifted for Barbara. She felt successful in her job as well as in her relationships with her colleagues and her boss.

This example also illustrates an important aspect of attitudes. Often, unsupportive attitudes develop because an underlying focus, skill, or habit isn't in place. Addressing these as Barbara did, can make all the difference in the world.

Answer the following questions in your journal:

- What attitudes do I have that support me at my Highest and Best?
- What attitudes do I have that drag me down to my lowest and worst?
- How did these attitudes develop?
- How do these attitudes impact me personally and professionally?
- How might I develop more supportive attitudes?

## Habits

**Habits are what you do automatically with little thought or effort.**

Habits are what you do automatically with little thought or effort. They may involve any combination of your mental, physical, or emotional selves. Habits are predictable and comfortable. Your habits activate as a result of your initiation, your responses, or your rituals.

Good habits support who you are and what you are doing. They foster the growth and development of your hopes, dreams, and aspirations. They contribute to your success and your endeavors as well as your daily life.

**Good habits support who you are and what you are doing.**

Bad habits have just the opposite effect. They detract from who you are and from your efforts to create what you want. They limit you from using your potential, interfering and sabotaging you along the way.

Coaches are always on the lookout for habits that are essential to success; helping to identify, establish, and maintain them. Counterproductive habits need to be weeded out. You must also be careful not to classify a habit as right or wrong as it isn't always as cut and dry as it may seem. You must look at more than just the habit to determine if it is an interference or not. Factors such as surrounding circumstances, personality styles, and the individual's goals and objectives must be considered. An essential habit for one may be interference for another.

For Earl, a senior vice president of a large manufacturing company, the habit of routine is critical to his success. He has an unyielding allegiance to his routines. They feel safe and secure. He's able to access more creative energy when he's in a routine, and his accomplishments prove it.

For Barry, another senior vice president within the same organization, routine is just this side of death. When forced into a routine, he feels stifled and suffocated to the point of not being able to be productive. Barry needs variety and lots of it. With it, his creativity and productivity soar.

Because you spend so much of your life in your habits, you may find that changing one habit may create a domino effect in changing other habits.

*Changing Habits*

Tracy, married mother of two, enjoyed going out after her children were in bed. Four or five evenings a week, she met friends for drinks at a local hangout. They always smoked cigarettes, something she never did in front of her children. Tracy decided to quit smoking. This affected her motivation to go out to bars as frequently. With more time in the evenings, she joined a swim club that she enjoyed with her family twice a week. The additional exercise and reduction of alcohol helped Tracy maintain her weight after she quit smoking. She was amazed at how changing just one habit created a positive domino effect. And for Tracy and her family, the effect was beautiful.

When creating a new habit, look around and see if there are related habits that need your attention.

Steve decided to develop the habit of taking a brisk walk every morning upon rising. He anticipated the results of this practice to be quite favorable. He would be more fit, happier, alert, and ready to start his day. The first few mornings were great. Soon, though, he was too tired to get up early enough to get his walk in. Steve had neglected to consider another habit: staying up late at night. That pattern developed because of another habit: a couple of hours of TV each night. When he cut back on his TV consumption, his bedtime changed and his daily walks became sustainable.

Habits often rely on other habits that depend on other habits. You might have to go several habits deep to understand the full consequences of a new habit. There may be other changes needed to be successful. If you organize your desk but are in the habit of leaving things out to remind you to do them, you are going to create a new problem. That is, of course, unless you create a new habit of using an effective time-management system that helps you keep track of your "to do's" so you don't fall victim to the "out of sight, out of mind" trap.

In your journal, answer the following questions about your personal and professional life:

- What are my best habits?
- What are my worst habits?
- What habits do I wish I had?
- What habits do I wish to change?
- What do I need to do to change or create habits to support me?

Now let's put the POWERFUL FOUR together.

First, make sure there is an appropriate focus that can be maintained and shifted as necessary. Then, identify the skills needed to be successful and whether they are sufficient or if they need to be developed or purchased. Next identify and support the attitudes and habits that will foster growth, development, and success.

Although these steps appear to be very linear, your ability to move around these Powerful Four as needed makes this a very dynamic tool.

With the POWERFUL FOUR in mind, let's spend a little more time with Dana, the owner of the troubled physical therapy business. Let's observe the inner play and movement between focus, skills, attitudes, and habits.

As you recall, we left Dana focusing on her desk, practicing the skills of desk management. She was cultivating an attitude that embraced order while developing a habit of keeping a neat and orderly desk. With that in place, we moved her focus to her thinking. To create order and calmness in her thinking, I taught her time management skills, fostering an attitude that she always had time for the important things in her business and her life. This focus, skill, and attitude became another habit.

Next, we moved to meetings. I wanted Dana to focus on generating movement and necessary organizational corrections through her meetings. She needed meeting management skills and she got them. She developed the habit of leading meetings that were focused and productive. She also made a habit of tracking and following up on all the assignments she made to her staff, in and out of meetings. She developed and encouraged an attitude that everyone had a part in the success of the operation. Her business began to turn around. Soon, key employees began modeling her desk management. She taught a few of them her new time management skills. Unlike before, accountability became expected. In short, Dana was taking control of her organization and leading by example.

A few employees who had found power in the chaos fought the changes and were quickly recognized as troublemakers. Ultimately, they couldn't handle Dana's newfound approach and quit. The remaining staff began to blossom. Some came around faster than others. Eventually, they all did. Within a short time, Dana had a plan to address the next set of problems that were causing them trouble. Using her newly developed focus, skills, attitudes, and habits, she implemented her plan and saved her business.

Dana won the admiration of their banker who had thought she would destroy her business. He had never seen an organization turn around so quickly. He happily restructured her loans, giving her the time and support she needed to succeed.

The Powerful Four Method is a helpful mental organizing tool for coaching, personally and professionally. It will help you gain a better understanding of yourself and others, specifically and in general. It also provides a wonderful structure to assist you in identifying the specific elements as well as actions needed for success. All things being equal, if these four things are in place, you can't help but succeed.

No matter who you are or what your role is—coach, business owner, executive, professional, teacher, parent, student, worker or individual—you can successfully use the Powerful Four to help create the shifts, changes, and growth you are looking for to lead you to your Highest and Best.

minister • judge • elder • manager • cousin • counselor • doctor • past

CHAPTER 3

# Listen, Mirror, Path, Floodlight Method

*The Anatomy of a Coaching Conversation*

*While using my POWERFUL FOUR,* I observed a pattern in the conversations I had with my clients that helped them develop into the people they wanted to be, doing the things they wanted to do, at their Highest and Best. This method has been introduced to and adopted by new and veteran coaches worldwide since the early 1990's. Instantly seeing the beauty and ease of this method, they saw how easily it could be adapted to a wide variety of coaching styles, blending nicely with other valuable tools. For some coaches, it provided a simple explanation of what they were already doing. Others began using it as a road map, enhancing the method with their own style. Play with it in your conversations. You just might be surprised by the results!

To illustrate this method, I would like to start with a theatrical explanation of a coaching conversation I use when teaching new coaches about the process of coaching.

*Imagine you and your client are on a stage. The house lights are dark. You're sitting center stage facing each other. There is a single light on your client. They are telling you about themselves. You listen intently without judgment, without preconceived ideas. You listen deeply to their words, feelings, and ideas. You listen with discernment, looking for what is hidden. You listen for clarity. Your client finishes. The single light fades.*

*You and your client stand. To your right, a light appears to reveal a mirror. You walk your client up to the mirror, gently placing them in front of it. You stand slightly behind their right shoulder so you can whisper into their ear. You begin to talk with your client about what you see in them, who they are as a person, the talents they have, and the challenges they face. You stay at the mirror until you are both in agreement. The light over the mirror fades.*

*From the middle of the stage, there is a new, more powerful light. A beam is projected high into the blackness of the audience. A path appears. You and your client move toward the light. Together, standing shoulder to shoulder, you look upon their vision. You put your arm around them as if to give strength. What you both are seeing is their potential future. You talk about what you see: the opportunities, the milestones, the obstacles, and the roadblocks. Some places are clear; others are fuzzy. You each see parts the other cannot see. Together, you know enough to understand where your client is going and what's in store for them. The journey looks exciting. Your client turns to you, looking for advice. "Where shall I begin?" they ask.*

*As if by magic, a floodlight has been cast upon the first few feet of their path, illuminating your client's next steps, the steps that will take them on a journey to their Highest and Best.*

The four phases of the coach conversation are straightforward. Listen, mirror what you've heard, recognize their path, and put a floodlight on their next step.

**The four phases of the coach conversation are straightforward. Listen, mirror what you've heard, recognize their path, and put a floodlight on their next step.**

This method keeps you focused in the right direction. By using this simple structure, you can learn a great deal about another person on many different levels. It directs you to grasp the essence of who they are, where they are going, and what they will need to get there, whether it is in the grand scheme of their lives or a simple daily concern.

Now, let's take a look at what happens behind the scenes to discover what makes this method so powerful.

## Listen

The first step in listening is to provide a safe space for the person. This is a place in which one can reveal oneself, totally and utterly, without fear of judgment. Encourage them to share as much as they can about themselves. Ask questions to understand. Don't use your questions to lead them to a particular answer. Help them explore themselves. Be fully present. Your listening will become finely tuned.

**The first step in listening is to provide a safe space for the person.**

Listen to what they say, how they say it, and their selection of words and ideas. You will hear their emotions, their preferences, and their focus. As you listen, you will hear their attitudes and beliefs. You will even hear their expectations. You are beginning to get an idea of who they are and what makes them tick.

**Listen to what they say, how they say it, and their selection of words and ideas.**

If you're talking with your client in person, you can gather even more information from the way they dress, the way they move, or how they sit. Watch the changes in their eyes as they talk, their hand motions, even the way they handle their belongings. The wealth of information you can receive in just a few minutes with someone is incredible. You can be quick to understand them if you use another source of information: your inside self.

**You will hear their attitudes, beliefs, and expectations.**

Your inside self talks to you, making comments, statements, and posing questions. You might also see pictures and images, often appearing to be unrelated. You may have emotional and physical reactions. When you pay attention to this source, you are doing what I call "inside listening." If you are sensitive to what your inside-self tells you, you will have many more clues to understand your client at a deeper, more profound level. The art of blending your inside and outside listening makes the coaching process very quick and effective.

**Your inside self talks to you, making comments, statements, and posing questions.**

Emily came to me looking for help in her quest to find her true self and her true vocation. Her self-esteem and energy were low. Her progress was slow but steady. We focused on clearing out some of the clutter in her life including a man and some belongings. She was even ready to leave her part-time job as a bookkeeper if only she could figure out what kind of work she wanted to do. One thing that confused me was her delight in creating unusual outfits with clothes from thrift stores. She was a woman of considerable means and could have easily afforded new clothes.

**The art of blending your inside and outside listening makes the coaching process very quick and effective.**

Right before one of her appointments, my inner voice said, "Put up a drawing easel, give her some colored markers, play some classical music, and ask her to draw to the music." I wasn't sure why I was being directed this way, but I soon found out. What I saw surprised me. It was not so much from what she drew; but in her body, the way she held herself, the way she moved. She had confidence. Her style of dress suddenly made sense: she was an artist!

Emily had never said one word about art. It was never a consideration. When I told her what I saw, she saw it immediately. Sure enough, it was a fundamental part of her. She signed up for art classes. Within no time, she held her first art exhibit, created a faux finishing business and shifted her efforts at work from bookkeeper to brochure designer.

As she became aware of her artistic self, Emily's self-esteem improved. She was no longer lost or tired. Her new focus has made an incredible difference in her life. Simply by following my inside messages, I was able to help Emily discover so much about herself and her true vocation.

We all have an inner listening ability to varying degrees. Let's spend a few minutes with an exercise that can help you recognize and develop this skill.

**We all have an inner listening ability.**

In two sentences, I'm going to tell you about someone you don't know. Take a moment and make a note of what you know about this person from your outside listening and what you know about them from your inside listening. Remember to pay attention to all your internal words, pictures, feelings, and reactions.

Okay, let's try it.

*Mark is a surgical assistant for a local veterinarian. He and his wife want to put up a privacy fence in their backyard.*

- Stop and make your list of what you know about Mark from both your inside and outside listening.

Now let's go over some of the possible things you can readily figure out. Mark is a man. He is employed. He doesn't have far to go to work. He is highly specialized. He works with his hands. He's married. He and his wife want privacy in their backyard, and they want a fence.

What you know for sure is from your outside listening; the facts came from the two sentences above.

What did you hear, feel, or see inside yourself?

Here's what three coaches said after hearing these two sentences about Mark. "When you mentioned his occupation, I immediately thought of my sister's animals. She has a dog and a cat." Another said, "For some reason, I flashed on my aunt, who always seemed to have trouble with her neighbors." Still another coach said, "I began feeling the same stress and tension I had when I worked in surgery." Each of these clues came from the coaches' inside listening.

You might have heard the following from your inside listening. Mark loves animals. He has animals at home. He and his wife own their home. They spend time in their backyard. They do not want their neighbors or anyone else to look in their yard. Mark loves to do projects using his hands. By the time he gets home, he just wants to be alone. Their house backs up to a street. Mark is having trouble with his neighbors.

Let's check our accuracy. I know these things about Mark: Mark and his wife are newlyweds. They have a dog and a cat. They recently bought their home. He does carpentry projects around the house. He is extremely neat and tidy. He works a twelve-hour shift, four days a week. He spends time relaxing on their back patio. There is a hot tub in their backyard they frequently use. The house backs up to an alley. They like the neighbor on one side of them; they don't like the neighbor on the other side. So, how'd you do?

Some of your most powerful questions will come from your ability to tune into your inner voice. Let your questions be guided not only by the obvious but the ones that may not make any sense. You can find a great deal of information from these internally motivated questions, gaining much-needed information and personal insight during this process.

In summary, the act of being fully present allows you to learn more about the person you are having a conversation with or coaching. By blending the information you receive from both outside and inside yourself, you gain access to more profound, meaningful information making your coaching quick and affective and your conversations more meaningful. In the process, you give a most incredible gift: being heard.

## Mirror

In the second step of this method, you walk your client up to the mirror. You help them see who they are. You share with them how they appear to you from many different angles. This significant challenge represented in the theatrical version has you positioned behind them, slightly to the right so that you can whisper in their ear. If you are to be understood, you must present your findings in a manner they can hear. They need space to see and evaluate what you are saying to them. Your close position also indicates that you want their feedback.

**Share with them how they appear to you from many different angles.**

As you paint this picture of them, check with them:

- "Are you with me?"
- "Do you see what I'm pointing out?"
- "Do you want to add something?"
- "Do I have something wrong?"
- "Do you have any comments, questions or concerns?"

Observe how they appear. Are they happy, afraid, skeptical? For many, it may be the first time in their lives they have had the experience of being truly heard and acknowledged. They may have never experienced someone giving them information about themselves without judgment or ulterior motives. It is through this process that they develop a deeper awareness of who they are. Being seen, heard, and accepted are primary and fundamental pieces to building self-esteem and deepening self-awareness. They develop naturally and effortlessly.

In the beginning, place your focus on the positive. These are not empty compliments but true feedback about their positive attributes. You want them to increase their confidence and strength for their upcoming work. As for the things that aren't positive, you'll deal with those in time. Once their confidence is strengthened, it's much easier to clean up the areas holding them back.

**In the beginning, place your focus on the positive.**

When you discuss what you see, ask them if they agree with you. Their answers will range from completely to not at all. Where you go from here depends upon where you end up on the continuum between these points. When you both agree, you can move on. When your perceptions are different, you may need a bit more information or to adjust either their or your perception a bit. Perhaps an entirely different perspective is required.

Peter, a coach from the Midwest, began his coaching with me by saying, “I’m not very good at coaching. I used to be, but I’m not now.” As I listened to Peter describe his coaching approach and the results his clients experienced, it was evident that he was an excellent coach. Unfortunately, he had begun to believe that to be a good coach required abandoning his own natural style and adopting the style and methods of the coach-training program he was attending.

Peter had begun to believe that there was only one way to coach and he couldn’t do it. I gently walked him up to the mirror to see how this belief was stifling him. When I focused him on his positive attributes, he began to remember who he really was. He regained his appreciation of himself as a truly gifted coach. He could choose to adopt the ideas and methods from the training program that served him and leave the rest behind. Today, Peter coaches from his strengths and enjoys a successful and fulfilling coaching practice.

Sometimes, the pictures you see so clearly are fuzzy to your clients. They may have a sense that you are right but aren't quite sure. In these instances, you may give them more information, or you might ask them to trust you. Over time, you help them develop clarity about themselves through experiences and exercises.

There are times they may say, "Nope. You don't have that right at all." The good coach will say, "Okay. You tell me what's right." It's important for you to accept that you don't have to be right. Your acceptance of not being right can actually be very helpful to your clients. It's another measure of your acceptance of them and your own fallibility.

Sometimes valuable information is buried within the person you are coaching, and it needs a little help getting out. By giving them your impressions, they have something to push against. They want so much to be understood that they will reach deeper inside of themselves until they can find what is truly right for them. Sometimes their answers are very different from what they told you the first time around.

What happens when you realize that the individual either doesn't see what you see or they don't have a good picture of themselves? One thing you can do is employ tools that will help them develop an understanding of who they are.

Here are a couple of ideas.

Send them on a fact-finding mission asking their family, friends, and colleagues questions that could give them an insight into themselves. Questions like,

- What are my best characteristics and strengths?
- Where do you see me going?
- What do you see me doing with my life?

Ask them to make notes about what they learned. From there, have them observe themselves for a week from a new perspective created from the feedback they received.

Journaling provides another means of self-discovery. You can ask them to respond to a series of questions such as:

- What did I do today that I feel good about?
- What have been the significant events in my life?
- What accomplishments am I proud of?
- What would I like to accomplish in the future?
- What makes me feel proud?
- What do I know about myself as a result of a good experience I've had?
- What do the answers to the previous questions tell me about myself?

These questions, designed for internal discovery, helped my client Albert realize that while he was a successful dentist, his love for teaching was overlooked. I encouraged him to pursue his passion and aptitude for teaching inside and outside of his dental practice. He quickly found an opportunity to teach at the dental school and added an extensive dental health educational component to his dental practice. Albert transformed his once mildly fulfilling dental profession into a daily "shouting from the rooftops with joy" experience.

There are a variety of personality and vocational assessment tools that may help you gain clarity. Some coaches like to use personality and interest assessment tools such as the Myers-Briggs and the DISC (a profile which evaluates Dominance, Influence, Steadiness and Conscientiousness).

Relationship coach Maria used the DISC to help Sherry and Victor gain insight and understanding of themselves and one another. The "third party" explanation of their fundamental personality traits and responses helped them see one another in a new light. Maria used the information she gleaned from the report to help them communicate and support each other in a way they previously had not thought possible.

Whatever tools or ideas you use, helping someone know themselves better is a significant step in coaching.

This step can sometimes be a bit tricky when there is a huge problem that needs to be addressed. Early in my coaching career, I had to tell three different clients some very tough observations: a psychiatrist that he needed therapy, a minister that he had lost his spiritual connection, and a positive thinking motivational speaker that his negativity was ruining his business. To be their Highest and Best, they needed to take actions that may have seemed odd considering their professions. All three men were able to hear me and take the steps they needed to correct their problems because they felt safe, heard, understood, and honored.

One last thought. Some folks will explain to you very clearly where you're wrong, and in their opinion, what is right. If you see the picture they paint, you continue. If you don't, you have a new challenge. There are times that, no matter how much you or the individual tries, you just don't get it. This is an appropriate time to help them find another coach or, if you think something is amiss, you might want to suggest they see a therapist.

The point of mirroring is to help them see themselves at their Highest and Best and in the possibilities, great and small. As you saw, sometimes this is easy, and sometimes it takes more time and resources. Either way, you

**The point of mirroring is to help them see themselves at their Highest and Best and in the possibilities, great and small.**

must reach this awareness together. It's a necessary piece of the coaching processes.

## Path

So, here we are again, back on our stage. You have listened to your client, gently walked them up to the mirror, talked about who they are. Now it's time to talk about their path: who they're becoming and where they're going. In my theatrical example, the coach stands shoulder to shoulder with their client looking at their path.

This symbolism represents the role of the coach. Your job is not to be ahead of them. You don't pull them forward, nor do you encourage them to catch up. You don't stand behind them pushing them on their way. Your job is to journey with them, discussing their path, looking at what lies ahead.

The symbolic gesture of gently putting your arm around them represents the strength and courage you give them. They are not alone as they travel their path. You will be there for them when it's easy or tough, rewarding or disappointing. You are their coach. The path may appear suddenly or gradually. Maybe it's been there all along, and now it's the first time they've seen it. The path may be about your client's overall future, a specific area of their life, or a particular aspect of either.

As you are looking at their path, you talk about where they are going and who they are becoming. You describe their journey and the kinds of experiences they might have. You celebrate potential opportunities and milestones. You evaluate the obstacles and the road-blocks. You paint a picture of something in their future, very near or very far away.

**As you are looking at their path, you talk about where they are going and who they are becoming.**

Their reactions may vary. Some may say, "Oh, my gosh. You see that? So do I!" Something in them sparkles. It may motivate them, relieve them, or even scare them. Either way, it will definitely move them. Sometimes, you can see their path, but they can't. You use one of the same processes you used when mirroring. You give them more information. You shift their perspective and ask them to trust you.

But what if you can't see the path the person is describing? Now you have a new challenge. Perhaps they think it's their path because it's the one they believe they should follow.

One such client was Monica who had asked me to help her improve her business. As we went through this process, we ran into trouble seeing her path. She struggled to define it to me. All she could see was that she just had to make her business work.

As she was explaining all the "shoulds" of her path, I began to see something completely different. I saw her with children. Children had never come up in our conversation, so I was a little confused. But trusting my inside listening, I asked her if she would take on a funny assignment: would she be willing to spend a few mornings observing several grade school classes? She took me up on the idea and was surprised by what she learned.

Monica immediately realized she was on the wrong path. She sold her business, one she never really wanted. She enrolled in a teacher's training program, and now has years of teaching under her belt. Once in the training program, I received a lovely note from her husband. "Thank you. I feel like my wife is back. I have never seen her so happy."

All right, but what if you're wrong about their path? Well, the same thing happens as when you mirror. You accept that you are not always right and you admit it to the person you are coaching. You also realize that not being right might help them discover what is right.

Virginia, a disillusioned attorney, wanted help in discovering her professional path. She was frustrated with her own efforts and just couldn't get clear. Under my direction, I asked her to focus on a path that had made sense from what we had discussed. It turns out that it was the wrong path. Shortly after that, I received a very forceful letter from her telling me under no uncertain terms that I didn't know what I was talking about; this was entirely the wrong direction for her. She described in great detail a completely different direction that had never come up in our discussion.

I called her and told her I was delighted for her; she had accomplished what she'd set out to do. At first, she was quite surprised by my reaction. But as we talked, she began to understand how starting down the wrong path had actually helped her see the right path. It gave her something to react to, something to push against. By the end of the call, she thanked me for helping her accomplish in only two weeks what she had unsuccessfully tried to do for several years. A year later, I received a holiday card from Virginia with a note describing how much she loved her new profession.

Another possible problem is that no matter how hard we try, we are unable to see the path they see. As in mirroring, if it persists, chances are the best thing we can do is encourage them to find another coach or therapist who can help them.

We have now looked at the person's path. We have discussed what we have seen, the opportunities and the potential roadblocks or obstacles. Some will be relatively easy for them to handle. Others may be a bit more challenging, requiring a confidence boost or some additional help from new skills or an outside resource. By and large, these things can be easily handled.

From this perspective, you may say to them, "You make a few adjustments; you may have to do some things that are a little uncomfortable, a little scary or cost you some money. Whatever it is, I believe in you, and I'll be there to help you."

There also may be some pretty formidable obstacles that may, in fact, stop them from moving forward. These barriers should be discussed in depth. If they should choose to continue down this path, a contingency plan may be in order.

David was developing a new business that had a small risk of being in violation of an employment agreement he had signed. While he didn't think that a court would find him in breach of the contract, it was evident that the owner of the company he had worked for would try to stop him. As we progressed in the development of his business, we always kept an eye on this potential obstacle. We talked at length about the possible cost of a court battle to his new business, his family, and himself.

I encouraged a contingency plan, and David complied. He negotiated a short-term contract to sell equipment to his industry, keeping him in front of his future customers. The owner managed to create a significant legal roadblock. He stopped David from moving forward with his business with a restraining order until the case could be heard in court some months later.

David's preparations for this moment were in place. His legal counsel was prepared and ready for action. His alternative employment plan would see him through the battle mounted against him. His dreams stayed intact. The ensuing legal battle took almost a year to complete. During this time, David's contingency plan enabled him to support his family and handle his legal fees. He ultimately won the right to proceed. David was now back in the game, successfully pursuing his dreams of owning his own business.

Those you coach, however, may choose another path. The choice is theirs. Respect their responsibility for determining their path. It is your job to hang in there with them, be present with them, and help them make the best decisions at each step. Sometimes you get to celebrate with them; sometimes you help them pick up the pieces and move on. When you are in a coaching role, you're not attached to their choices or the results—they are theirs and not yours.

One final thought about path work. The choice of paths and how they are navigated can, and often do, have significant implications in many areas of one's life. Be it yours or someone else's, it is important to think about how a particular path will impact other aspects of life before determining how best to proceed.

Shortly after his twin daughters were born, Paul was considered for a promotion. While the new position included a substantial raise as well as increased status, it also included more hours and 30 percent travel. After several values-centered discussions with his wife, Paul withdrew his name from consideration. He realized the promotion would have taken far too much away from his family at this time, particularly his very young daughters. Paul's values were clear. He had stayed true to what was most important to him and his family and was ultimately rewarded with a wonderful family-friendly promotion he enthusiastically accepted.

**The choice of paths and how they are navigated can, and often do, have significant implications in many areas of one's life.**

Doing path work is fundamental to all coaching. It can be used to help understand something as broad as one's professional life to determining what a change in attitude might bring. It allows you to see where they are going so you can help them plan their next steps.

## Floodlight

In the final scene, you're looking at the client's path together. Suddenly a floodlight appears to illuminate their next steps. Using your inner listening for ideas and guidance, you talk with them about what happens next, together identifying the next step(s).

In professional coaching, the steps someone agrees to take between coaching sessions becomes their homework. Their homework could be any number of things from an attitude-changing exercise to focusing on a new idea. It might be taking a concrete action like outlining a business plan or cleaning off their desk.

To give you an understanding of what these steps might entail, let's look at three common characteristics:

- First, the actions are often related to the previous three stages of seeing and knowing who they are, describing who they are, becoming who they want to be, and/or doing what they want to do.
- Second, they're often about one or more of the Powerful Four: Focus, Skills, Attitudes, or Habits.
- Third, these steps generally require one or more of the following: a change in thinking or attitude, a shift in behavior, or taking a particular action.

Sometimes, your inner messages for homework may not make sense to you. It is important to honor these messages. They can have life-changing consequences, or they can help clear the way for success.

Marcia, an interior decorator, hired me as her business coach. Although she was struggling with the few existing clients she had, she still wanted her business to grow. We began with the essential self-management tools of time and project management. While this helped her become more organized and efficient, it didn't address her desire to bring far more creativity to her practice that she had to date.

As we moved to the floodlight, I kept seeing an image of her sitting in a park sketching. As we looked at what she was to do next, we saw her need to rest in a quiet, peaceful place. We also saw that she needed to coax out her creativity. Her first assignment, inspired by the picture in my mind, was for her to sketch one hour a day in a peaceful park. She followed through with that homework and all the other odd assignments that followed. The process worked. Marcia ultimately gained more access to her creative powers. Her belief in herself soared, as did her ability to follow through on promises with herself and her clients. In time, she developed a very successful practice featuring a unique approach to interior design, with a waiting list of clients.

Remember Monica, businesswoman turned schoolteacher? What I saw in her floodlight didn't make sense to me, either. I just trusted the images I was receiving, and magic happened. My inner guidance has never let me down. I bet yours won't let you down either.

The point of coaching is to foster clarity that results in movement toward their Highest and Best. Many clients do their homework and make the progress they need. Some never do it, but they change nonetheless. Then, other clients neither do their homework nor progress. There are many reasons for this. Perhaps the person does not have enough space in their life for coaching.

Another reason someone might not do their homework is that they don't really want to do the work to grow or they aren't capable. Coaches have a new challenge when their client thinks that somehow by showing up for their session and paying a fee, the coach will do the work for them. It would be better to discontinue these relationships. Perhaps it would be appropriate to refer them to someone trained in more in-depth work.

Sometimes coaches find themselves working with someone who doesn't have a solid functional base. When this happens, it is often better to refer them to a therapist. Professionally, I am willing to do a little dusting and cleaning, but no excavation. We all have stuff we need to clean up. But we need to let the people who are trained in dealing with the heavy-duty stuff handle deep-seated problems.

When teaching coaches, I like to use the the bell curve to create an image of the mental health continuum as a guide.

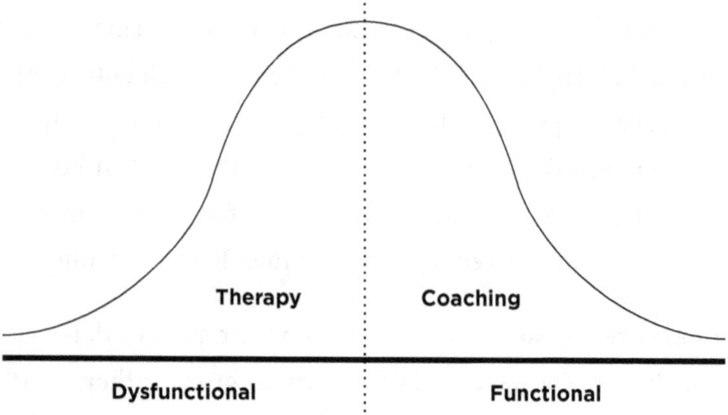


Coaching relationships work best when the person is somewhere near to or to the right of functional. Anyone on the left of functional would do far better in therapy or a remedial program. All professional coaches should be familiar enough with possible mental health dysfunctions such as anxiety, depression, addictions, and personality disorders to know when it is appropriate to refer individuals to a mental health professional. Coaching someone to accept mental health help is some of the most important work of all.

Luckily, the majority of clients takes the information from the floodlight phase and do make progress, leading them to their Highest and Best. They understand that the steps identified in their floodlight are for them to do. Their homework makes sense to them, and it works. Through this process, they learn to see what is next in many areas of their life, with and without a coach.

You don't have to be a professional coach to have a great coaching conversation. Now that you've explored the Listen, Mirror, Path, Floodlight Method, I invite you to try it yourself.

Think back to a recent conversation you have had and answer the following questions:

**You don't have to be a professional coach to have a great coaching conversation.**

- How well did I listen?
- Did I use my inside listening?
- Did I mirror back what I heard?
- Did I help them discover their paths and light their way?
- Did I see them at their Highest and Best?

Try it on yourself as well. You might be surprised at how you support yourself or how you are hurting yourself. Take a minute and journal your responses:

- How well am I listening to myself?
- Mirroring back to myself, what am I seeing, thinking, and feeling?
- Can I see my path? What is it?
- Can I light my own way?
- What are my next steps?

You may discover that you've already been doing this naturally. Or, it may be an excellent new tool to help you see things differently…for yourself and others. You may decide you want or need a coach or even a therapist. You just might take to this approach so well that you consider becoming a coach yourself. You never know until you try!

The Listen, Mirror, Path, Floodlight Method is designed to take us to our Highest and Best. By incorporating these steps in your conversations, you will be guided to listen carefully to what is being said and what you hear inside yourself, acknowledging what is good about yourself and others, understanding and supporting the path, and identifying what needs to be done. You will see what is possible or what is missing and have an action plan to make dreams become a reality.

**The Listen, Mirror, Path, Floodlight Method is designed to take us to our Highest and Best.**

To your Highest and Best!

CHAPTER 4

# Combining Techniques: Coaching Conversation and The Powerful Four

*Any coaching tool or technique worth its salt should blend nicely with the other tools in your toolbox.*

*To understand* how tools can work together, let's combine the mental organizing tool, *The Powerful Four: Focus, Skills, Attitudes, and Habits* with the *Coaching Conversation: Listen, Mirror, Path, Floodlight Method* into a format you can refer to when you practice coaching. As you go through, add your own questions and insights. Make it your own! You can even use it to wrestle down a challenge you are facing.

Now, let's merge them and see what happens.

**Focus** is where one is looking, where one is headed, where one is putting one's energy. The ideal focus is clear, strong, steady, and flexible, moving from the big picture to detail, detail to the big picture and points in between, and appropriate to their path.

## Coaching

*Listen:* Determine what the person is focusing on and if it's supporting their goals and objectives. Feel free to ask clarifying questions. Be careful not to look for an answer that fits your preconceived notion of what their focus should be. This is about them, not you, (unless, of course, you are self-coaching).

- What is their focus?
- Is their focus strong and stable or does it bounce around?
- Have they focused appropriately?
- Do they have the focus necessary to achieve their goals, objectives, and tasks?
- Are they able to hold their focus?
- Is their focus of interest to them?

*Mirror:* Tell them what you hear about their focus. Answer the following questions one at a time or alternating in a conversational manner. Work until there is agreement.

- What is their focus?
- Where do they think they are focusing?

- Do they want a different focus?
- Is their focus clear, steady, or does it move around?
- Does their focus support their Highest and Best?
- Discuss until there is agreement.

*Path:* Talk with them about the road they are taking and the outcome they will get as a result of their focus.

- What is the likely outcome of their focus?
- Does their focus support their stated goals and objectives?
- If they are in a group, does it support the group's goals and objectives?
- What changes or adjustments can you recommend?
- Discuss until there is agreement.

*Floodlight:* Together determine the next steps. Always give the person a chance to come to these ideas first.

- Determine what actions are needed to strengthen their focus, or to change their focus to a more appropriate one.
- Identify the first three steps to help them gain, maintain, or strengthen their focus and get a commitment to acting on them with specific, measurable results.
- Discuss until there is agreement.

**Skills** are the knowledge, understandings, and abilities required to accomplish specific goals, objectives, or tasks. The skill-set needed may include technical, interpersonal, knowledge, and process. Does the person have the necessary skills and understanding to fulfill the goals, objectives, or tasks they are required or want to do?

## Coaching

*Listen:*

- Do they know what skills and knowledge are needed to be successful in their endeavors?
- Do they know how to discover the skills they need?
- Do they have the necessary skills, knowledge, and understanding of the skills needed to be successful in their situation or to accomplish their goals?

*Mirror:* Talk with the person about:

- Their skill-set and knowledge-base.
- Identify any strengths or weaknesses.
- What specific skills they need to address.
- Discuss until there is agreement.

*Path:* Talk with them about:

- How their current skill and knowledge base will impact their path.
- What skills and knowledge they need to improve, add, or obtain from others.
- If needed, creating an action plan for determining what skills or knowledge are needed.
- A plan for improving or acquiring skills and knowledge, and,
- A path that fits current skills available.
- Discuss until there is agreement.

*Floodlight:* Determine what next action(s) is/are needed.

- If unclear on skill requirements, learn what skills/ knowledge are needed to be successful in their endeavor.
- Sharpen their skills/knowledge.
- Develop new skills.
- Acquire skills from outside sources.
- Discuss until there is agreement.
- Identify the first three steps to help them gain, maintain, or strengthen their skills and get a commitment to acting on them, with specific, measurable results.

**Attitudes** are the mental and emotional positions from which one views the world. They can be supportive or detrimental. Attitudes influence the behavior of an individual and the quality of their contribution to themselves and others. Attitudes are the manifestation of underlying beliefs, values, intentions, and habit patterns.

Life-enhancing attitudes include self-responsibility, acceptance, appreciation/gratitude, truthfulness, and willingness. Life-destroying attitudes include self-pity, denial, rejection, narcissism, or inflated self-importance. Harmful attitudes are often so habitual that the individual does not recognize the effect of them.

## Coaching

*Listen:* Identify the person's attitudes:

- Are they enhancing or destroying?
- What is motivating or feeding their attitudes?
- What attitude does the person need in their situation to be successful?

*Mirror:* Help them understand:

- The attitudes they are displaying or communicating.
- How their attitudes are showing up in their life.
- How their attitudes are impacting how they see the world.
- Discuss until there is agreement.

*Path:* Help them to see:

- Attitudes that will support their goals/aspirations.
- The positive and negative impact their current attitudes will have on their journey.
- Which, if any, adjustments need to be made.
- Discuss until there is agreement.

*Floodlight:* Help them identify:

- If an attitude change is needed, choose one at a time, the most important or easiest to change. Create a game plan to help them create change and a plan for any attitude slips.
- If there is resistance, ask them to observe the attitude in action for a week and make a note of what they learn.
- Discuss until there is agreement.
- Identify the first three steps to help them gain, maintain, strengthen, or change their attitudes and get a commitment to acting on them with specific, measurable results.

Note and beware: Unhealthy attitudes often develop from deep-seated values, beliefs, or experiences that cannot be easily changed without the skill of a therapist or mental health professional. If you believe this is the case, your job, if you are a coach, is to guide them to the right help.

**Habits** are that which one does automatically, often with little thought or effort to initiate. They may involve any combination of our mental, emotional, or physical selves. Good habits support you and what you want to do. Bad habits detract from being your best and doing what you want. They limit you, interfering and sabotaging efforts. Changing one habit can create a cascading effect by changing other habits.

## Coaching

*Listen:* For the person's habits:

- Determine if these habits are supporting or detracting from what they are trying to accomplish.

*Mirror:* To the individual:

- Habits you have identified.
- The impact these habits are having on their life and success.
- Discuss until there is agreement.

*Path:* Help the person:

- Determine what habits support their goals/aspirations.
- See the positive and negative impact their current habits will have on their journey.
- Which, if any, adjustments need to be made.

- If habits need changing, create an overall game plan together to establish new habits and displace habits that don't serve them.
- Discuss until there is agreement.

*Floodlight:* Help them identify next steps:

- If a change in habit is needed, choose one at a time, the most important or easiest to change.
- Create a game plan to help them create change and a plan for any habit slips.
- If there is resistance, ask them to observe the habit in action for a week and make a note of what they learn.
- Identify the first three steps to help them gain, maintain, strengthen, or change their habits and get a commitment to acting on them with specific, measurable results.
- Discuss until there is agreement.

Note and beware: Unhealthy habits often develop from deep-seated values, beliefs, experiences that cannot change easily without the skill of a therapist or mental health professional. If you believe this is the case, your job, if you are a coach, is to guide them to the right help.

In summary, you can use The Powerful Four within the Coaching Conversation to guide meaningful discussions regarding any topic, issue, or problem. You are just looking and listening for different things.

Now that you have seen how these two methods can be blended, give it a try. You can add the tools and insights presented, individually or in combination, with your own skill-set. You will get to know yourself and others better, improve communications, and gain confidence to create the life you want. You just might be surprised at the quality of conversation, problem-solving, planning, and action that can happen from this approach.

Again, to your Highest and Best!

CHAPTER 5

# Your Standards and Boundaries

*Knowing, understanding, and activating your standards and boundaries are fundamental to achieving your Highest and Best.*

*Your personal standards*—high or low—are your set of rules defining what is important to you and what you commit yourself to maintain. They also describe your expectations of others. Ensuring the ongoing alignment between what you value and your thoughts, words, and deeds is dependent upon how well you establish and maintain your standards and the boundaries which protect them.

> **Standards are your set of rules defining what is important to you and what you commit yourself to maintain.**

Standards exist for everything in your life from the simple to the complex. They define your personal, professional, spiritual, political, and community life. Your personal standards, the ones that are yours to establish, focus on you: how you think, act, and what you say. They define how you work and play and how you care for yourself and others. They also describe how you expect to be treated by others.

Just to be clear, your personal standards and boundaries have nothing to do with the authority of an organization or society. They have nothing to do with morally correct or acceptable behavior determined by someone else. No, it is about your own set of rules, the ones you create consciously or unconsciously, based on what you value. They define what's important to you, in any and all areas of your life. You have the right to base them on whatever you choose.

When you're clear about your standards, you know how you want to think and act. You know how you want others to treat you and how you want to treat them. More specifically, you know your expectations as they relate to you, family, friends, community, work, and society. You know whether those expectations are being met or not.

By identifying your standards ahead of time, you know what is acceptable to you and what is not. Armed with this information, you are in a much better position to have clear and intentional boundaries anchored to your Highest and Best standards. You can be confident that your thoughts, words, actions, and responses to yourself and others serve you.

Specifically, boundaries protect your rules, supporting and protecting your standards for you and from you as well as others. Boundaries have feedback signals, giving you notice when your thoughts, words, or deeds or someone else's are threatening your standards. They let you know that you need to do something to support your standards. Stored within your boundaries, whether you are aware of them or not, are your responses to threats, good, bad, or indifferent. The good responses support you; the bad responses get you into trouble; the indifferent responses (meaning you don't bother to respond at all) can result in being walked all over.

**Boundaries protect your rules, supporting and protecting your standards for you and from you as well as others.**

I like to think of the standard as a pillar and the boundary as that which holds the standard securely in place. Healthy standards and boundaries are somewhat flexible and have some give. It's not a rigid experience. It's comfortable.

In the next diagram, the center space represents you and your standards. The inner circle represents the boundaries you set for yourself. The outer circle represents the boundaries you set for others. The area between the two rings represents your boundaries and contains your reactions to when they are crossed.

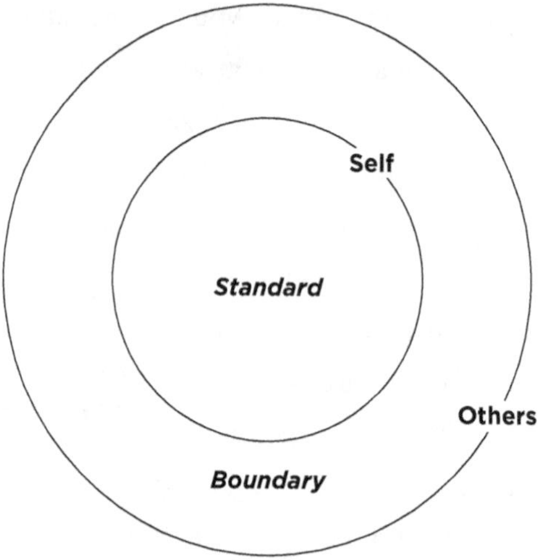


When someone or something crosses your outer boundary, you can expect to have an outward as well as inward response. The more violated your boundary, the stronger the impulse to respond to the threatened standard. It is the same with self-boundaries. If you are not acting or thinking in a manner that reflects your standards, you will have an internal reaction.

## Internal and External Boundaries at Play

Let's take a look at how this works with self-boundaries.

Jim, a financial planner, strives to help people develop strong financial portfolios. One of Jim's most important standards is to be good and kind to his clients. Jim knew that he was prone to bad attitudes that left him insensitive and less than kind to his clients. We worked to develop a response within his boundaries to handle his "less than optimal attitudes." When he found himself succumbing to one, he would call me so we could work to improve his attitude. Over time, I was able to help Jim recognize the symptoms of an impending attitude problem. He learned to redirect himself, often with physical exercise, to a better attitude. By doing so, Jim was able to keep himself in integrity with his standards.

I place a high value on learning. One of my standards is to say yes to new and different learning opportunities. This particular standard has opened many doors for me including traveling to Guatemala for dental outreach, being a chef for cancer survivors, and heading up a garden club. It is also a standard that can get me into a lot of trouble if I don't have proper boundaries around it. For example, my thirst for learning can lead to my taking on too many learning projects at one time. To help me navigate this little problem, I have established a "wait your turn" response in my boundaries so I won't overwhelm myself. It helps me stay with one primary focus at a time while satisfying my desire to learn.

Kristen has a standard of being on time. It is a standard she holds for herself and others. If she finds herself unable to meet her standard, she has an immediate reaction contained on her side of the boundary. First, if she's meeting someone, she notifies the person that she is going to be late. Second, she thinks back on what made her late and determines what adjustments she needs to make in her future planning.

If, on the other hand, Kristen was to meet someone and they are late, they are crossing her external boundary. She has a response to that as well. She expects them to notify her. If they don't, she asks them to do so in the future. If the person turns out to be chronically late, she has a different set of responses in her boundary circle.

Kristen may factor in their lateness in her own arrival time. She may choose not to set appointments with them, or she might bring something to occupy herself while she waits. Understanding that her responses reflect respect for herself, she allows herself to be gracefully guided in a manner that honors her Highest and Best as well as that of others.

Having clear standards and boundaries can help you be your Highest and Best in lowest and worse situations when your boundaries have been significantly crossed.

One night Liz was playing a quiet card game with a friend in a public living space at their apartment building. A young man entered and turned on three different televisions, all within yards of each other, all on different channels. He had taken only himself into account, neither asking nor apparently caring whether or not the chaotic noise would bother the women. His actions crossed significant boundaries for both Liz and her friend, aiming right for their standards of kindness and consideration.

Liz, usually very comfortable engaging in problem-solving and conflict resolution, found his actions and attitude getting the best of her. She was about to explain to him in no uncertain terms what she thought of his behavior when she turned to her friend and said, "Let's go." They gathered their things and found another quiet place to continue their card game.

**Having clear standards and boundaries can help you be your Highest and Best in lowest and worse situations when your boundaries have been significantly crossed.**

While moving to the next location, Liz was filled with gratitude for the guidance and protection of her standards and boundaries. Without them, she too could have become rude. The situation would have then escalated to a place that definitely would not have been her Highest and Best.

Richard, a CEO of an international, publicly-held company was getting beat up by his Board of Directors for not increasing the stock price. Charged with turning around the very company the Board had run into the ground, Richard was making tremendous progress remaking a workforce and work environment that would, in time, substantially increase the value of the organization and its stock price.

When I asked Richard about his standards and boundaries regarding interacting with his subordinates, he was quick to point out that he liked supporting others, giving them the benefit of the doubt whenever possible. He valued honest and direct exchanges. If a subordinate crossed his boundaries, he would sit them down and explain to them his expectations. Together, they would come up with a remedy. He was very comfortable setting standards and boundaries with those reporting to him.

His standards and boundaries with his Board, however, were another matter. Several Board members regularly barreled right through his boundaries, crushing his standards and his self-confidence. The criticism he faced was defeating. He wanted so much for them to see and acknowledge the progress he had made rather than focusing solely on profits for the stockholders.

As he examined his standards and boundaries, he realized he was working with two sets: one for his subordinates and one for his Board. He saw that he had excellent standards and boundaries for one and not the other.

He saw that he needed to set standards for how he received comments from the Board. He knew what he was doing and what he was accomplishing. He needed to keep that at the forefront of his mind. His standard of clearly seeing who he was and what he had accomplished needed to be protected. If he was attacked or unjustly criticized by Board members, he drew upon the automatic response he created in his internal boundaries to do a quick mental review of a few highlights of his incredibly successful career and the great strides he was making with this company to give the Board members what they wanted.

Richard also shored up his external boundaries when it came to the Board. Realizing that their first concern was the stock price, he went into the Board meetings ready for their comments. Richard understood that he needed to respond to their demand for increasing stock prices by bringing them back to the necessity of good business practices to keep the business viable over the long term.

He armed himself with excellent data, detailed descriptions of programs, and progress. Richard understood that it was his job to educate the Board and to focus them on the things that would ultimately get them what they wanted. If they raised their voices, he would pause, then speaking slowly and deliberately, address their concerns. Within his boundaries were responses that led him to educate his Board vs. react to them. In short, Richard developed a set of replies within his boundaries to deal with the Board members that moved everyone toward their Highest and Best.

### Setting high standards without being on a high horse

One way to be sure to avoid the high horse syndrome is to be keenly aware of your imperfections as they relate to your standards and boundaries and gracefully correct yourself. We all make mistakes. We all have times when our Highest and Best isn't that great, and it's hard to live up to our standards. Humbly, we set into action our responses when we do violate our standards.

My children were the recipients of my immediate and heartfelt apologies whenever I caught myself treating them in a manner that did not match my standards of motherhood. Sometimes, I would stop mid-sentence to correct myself. In doing so, I not only taught them that they deserved to be respected and treated fairly but to correct mistakes as soon as possible. We have a saying in our family that the best time to clean up a mess is as soon as it is made. You too can save yourselves from a great deal of hurt, guilt, and resentment by owning and correcting your mistakes as soon as possible.

**You can save yourselves from a great deal of hurt, guilt, and resentment by owning and correcting your mistakes as soon as possible.**

## Trouble in Paradise

Like anything else, standards and boundaries can go awry in a variety of ways. It might be you, it might be someone else, but it always causes trouble. It's a good idea to be familiar with them, lest you fall victim. Here are a few of the more obvious ones.

**Standards and boundaries can go awry in a variety of ways.**

### *Double Standards*

Double standards occur when there is one set of standards and boundaries for one group or person and a different set for another. This is often an attempt to control another group or person. The people who practice double standards are known as hypocrites. Authoritarians, dictators, cult leaders, and abusers are notorious for double standards. Common double standards in the workplace occur for women and minorities in pay, performance expectations, and promotions. Unfortunately, many of us experience and observe double standards in our work, families, religious organizations, businesses, and politics.

**Double standards occur when there is one set of standards and boundaries for one group or person and a different set for another.**

We can also see double standards playing out when we hold ourselves to standards that are higher than the ones we hold for others.

Ruth recently left an abusive relationship. She was concerned she would attract another such relationship. As we examined her standards, doing what she said she was going to do was high on her list. She expected others to do the same. When she examined her past relationship, she realized she had not protected this standard with any boundaries. When her boyfriend had failed to show up when he said he would, she didn't protect her standard by stating that if he couldn't keep his word, she wouldn't be interested in a relationship with him. Instead, she allowed him to make a few excuses and apologize. He proceeded to let her down—over and over again. For her part, Ruth failed to protect her standards of doing what she committed to and to taking care of herself in her relationships with men. As Ruth gained confidence in her ability to hold and protect her standards, she came to expect others to respect her standards as well. Ruth was surprised when she attracted a kind and considerate man who also respected her standards as well as his own.

### *Moving Standards and Boundaries*

Moving standards and boundaries are truly crazy-making, particularly for children and those who are in subservient positions. As the name implies, it is hard to know if the standards and boundaries one dealt with yesterday will be the same today or tomorrow.

**Moving standards and boundaries are truly crazy-making.**

Today, I am allowed to get cookies from the cookie jar by myself. Tomorrow, I am punished for the same act. The next day, I am told it is fine to get a cookie from the cookie jar on my own. I have no way of knowing what the rule will be tomorrow.

Odell was orphaned at a young age and spent the rest of his childhood moving from one foster home to another. Each placement brought a different set of rules and consequences that were difficult for him to grasp. They changed frequently and without warning, leaving him confused and frustrated. A troubled young man when he joined the military at seventeen, Odell found great comfort and much needed clarity and guidance in the military's written rules and clear consequences. Odell successfully served for 26 years, eleven tours of duty and has recovered from a serious head wound. He credits the military for turning him around.

### *Invisible Standards and Boundaries*

Sometimes a person has standards and boundaries that they are unaware of buried deep within them. Unfortunately, you only know when you or someone else has invisible standards and boundaries when they jump up and surprise you. Many a poor soul has landed in prison because of this serious problem.

A group of men are hanging out in a bar talking about women. Some are making very disparaging remarks that appear to be accepted by everyone until someone mentions a particular woman. Out of what feels like nowhere, someone is offended and responds violently. The police are called, and the offended fellow goes to jail.

### *Weak or Rigid Standards and Boundaries*

When your standards or boundaries are weak, it's hard to have much self-confidence or stand up for yourself. You don't know what you're shooting for and you are unable to defend yourself.

**When your standards or boundaries are weak, it's hard to have much self-confidence or stand up for yourself.**

On the other hand, if your standards and boundaries are rigid, you have no flexibility. You may find yourself alienating not only other people but also yourself from yourself. You might have set standards so high that no one could meet them. Then when they are crossed, all hell breaks loose. That does not get you to your Highest and Best.

### *Nonexistent Standards and Boundaries*

When you don't have standards and boundaries in general, or for something specific, you have no way of evaluating what is going on in the moment. This is the most difficult situation of all. You are left on your own, moment to moment, without any guidance. This creates havoc, and you end up at your lowest and worst.

Nate, a former Chicago gang member, turned contributing member of society, was looking for love. He met a beautiful young woman at a dance club. After a few compliments from her, he found himself explaining to her that with only $20,000 in savings, he didn't feel very financially secure. Armed with this information, the young lady started mentioning expensive things she would like. Not only was I surprised that Nate didn't appreciate his financial accomplishment, but by his lack of understanding of why he might want to keep that information to himself when meeting women. Nate was unaware of the idea of personal standards and boundaries.

Nate had had no formal education, no parental guidance, and no street knowledge of how standards and boundaries worked. As I explained this concept to him, he caught on quickly. As he started thinking about his standards for a partner, he realized he didn't want someone who was more interested in his money than in him. He also realized that he should keep his finances to himself until he had established a relationship based on mutual respect. He quickly saw how spending some time defining his standards and boundaries would not only keep him out of trouble in many areas of his life, but actually support him in becoming the kind of man he had always dreamed he could be.

Understanding, defining, and establishing good standards and boundaries for yourself and others provide you with ongoing guidance and information. You can see for yourself how well you are living your life according to your own rules. From a practical perspective, it allows you to make decisions quickly and easily and to have clean, clear responses to many of life's situations.

### Coaching for Standards and Boundaries

If you are coaching someone, you may see the need to examine standards and boundaries when the person brings forth something they are not satisfied with, whether it is a situation or experience with themselves or others. As they express their dissatisfaction, help them explore their standards and boundaries and if any adjustments need to be made. It is often helpful to use the standard and boundary circle to help them visualize this concept.

- Select a standard that seems to be the most appropriate for a chosen topic or concern.
- Ask them to define their standard, what it is, and why it is important to them.
- Once they are clear on their standard, a discussion for appropriate internal and external boundaries can take place.
- Remind them that their boundaries should be somewhat flexible.

The idea is to protect, not obliterate. The initial goal is to help the person understand the concept and focus on establishing and maintaining a meaningful standard and boundary. From there, practice and repeat.

Your turn to write in your journal:

- Choose something specific, personally or professionally, that is important to you.
- Using thoughts, words, and actions as a guide, make a list of the standards that support your Highest and Best as it relates to what you have chosen.
- What are the appropriate boundaries that will protect your standards both for you and from you and others?
- Observe yourself and see how focusing on your standards and boundaries support you (or don't!).
- Adjust as needed.
- Repeat until you are clear about your most important standards and the boundaries that protect them.

Practice and experience will teach you a lot about setting standards and boundaries. In the beginning, things may not go as smoothly as you would like. In time, you will learn to anticipate and navigate unintended responses. This is particularly true if you are setting boundaries with unhealthy people or those who have power over you.

Sometimes it can be hard to find the right way to make setting a boundary a win-win for everyone involved. If you do the best you can, think of the Highest and Best for all, and act with grace, dignity and respect for yourself and the other person, you will get the best possible outcome.

Knowing, understanding, and activating your standards and boundaries are fundamental to achieving your Highest and Best. They will provide you with ongoing guidance to create and maintain the type of life that honors you every step of the way.

**Knowing, understanding, and activating your standards and boundaries are fundamental to achieving your Highest and Best.**

To your Highest and Best!

CHAPTER 6

# Creating a Full and Fulfilling Life

*Support your Highest and Best life with clarity, space and development.*

*Now that you have spent some time* with the ideals of Highest and Best, the basic coaching conversation, a mental organizing tool, and standards and boundaries, I would like to share with you three basic concepts presented in the original *Simply Coaching* that I used to help coaches create full and fulfilling coaching practices. These same concepts can be applied to your life, your work, your play, and any endeavor you might undertake. These concepts are most powerful if you anchor them to your values, those things that are most important to you.

**I want to make it clear—you are not going for perfection, just *better*.**

I want to make it clear—you are not going for perfection, just *better*. And just in case you are not sure, let me make this perfectly clear: what follows is NOT A TO-DO LIST! Please let this soak in! If you don't, you are going to hate yourself and me! I repeat, THIS IS NOT A TO-DO LIST. It is just a GUIDE. Get it? A GUIDE to give you ideas, a way to sort through your life, regardless if your life is one big mess, a series of little messes, or damn near perfect.

**THIS IS NOT A TO-DO LIST. Get it? A GUIDE to give you ideas.**

Focus on getting better results in your life. Look for some ideas about the kinds of changes you might want to make in your life. If you evaluate yourself on your clarity, gifts, spaces, and development, you will get your own "State of the Me" report, your own mirror.

As I said, "Full and fulfilling" was a phrase I used to help coaches create and develop their practices. It may be a play on my own words, but it felt right to use them here as well. When coaching for a full and fulfilling practice or life at one's Highest and Best, I focus on three things: Clarity, Space, and Personal Development.

**Focus on getting better results in your life.**

Clarity:

- Your gifts and talents
- Those receiving your gifts

Space:

- Time, physical, mental, emotional, and spiritual

Personal Development:

- Learning and improving your focus, skills, attitudes, and habits
- Gaining knowledge, insight, and abilities

As you read these sections, think of them in the context of the coaching conversation. You are looking and evaluating. Listen, don't judge. Make notes. Then, mirror what you see. Be nice, be honest. Next, choose a path. Define it and create excitement. Then, put a light on the next steps—one or two, maybe three. Let them speak to you. Let the changes take hold and watch what happens. Next steps come…and you will see your strength, grace, and dignity grow as you focus on being your Highest and Best.

Let's dig deeper.

• futurist • grandfather • masseuse • politician • phlebotomist • ceo • c

CHAPTER 7

# Clarity

*The point of coaching*
*is to foster clarity that results*
*in movement toward their Highest and Best.*

*Clarity is the ability* to see both close and far with great understanding, accuracy, and insight. It provides vision, direction, inspiration, and motivation. Clarity is instrumental in becoming who you want to be and in creating the life you want to live. Wanting to achieve, maintain, and support clarity is often the motivation of those seeking personal, professional, or life coaching.

**Clarity is the ability to see both close and far with great understanding, accuracy, and insight.**

When you have clarity, you are free from confusion, clutter, or distraction. Seeing both the present and the future you are aiming for, you know what you want and understand what it will take to create it. You are realistic without hampering your drive or your creativity. You are aware of your strengths as well as your weaknesses. You are sure about your interests and stay true to them. The path to fulfilling your dreams will undoubtedly have its frustrations. Ultimately, with clarity, you are on your way to success.

**When you have clarity, you are free from confusion, clutter, or distraction.**

When you lack clarity, you lack direction. Your efforts fall short and you end up with too much, not enough, the wrong focus, the wrong people. It just doesn't work. You are confused. You start and stop, creating more confusion. You become frustrated, disillusioned; you get distracted. You complicate even the simplest things. Or, you don't even try. You are unsure of your options; getting what you want out of life is left to chance.

**When you lack clarity, you lack direction.**

You can think of clarity from the perspective for eyesight. Just as some people have 20/20 vision, some people seem to have 20/20 clarity. They can always see where they are going and what to do next. Others are farsighted. These people can only see where they are headed but can't see up close. They have challenges in knowing what to do next. There are still others who might be nearsighted. They can do close-up steps all day long, but don't exactly know where they are going or can't keep their eye on the "prize." And then, there are those who have 20/200 clarity. These folks are practically blind. They may always struggle with clarity, near or far or their clarity may be temporarily gone.

Sometimes lack of clarity comes from what is known as being "in the hallway." You may find yourself between opportunities when "one door closes, and you are waiting for the next door to open." Your normal clarity is elusive; you must wait to understand what is next for you. Like most people, being in the hallway is one of my least favorite places to be. Not sure of my next step or focus, I am restless and uncomfortable. I want the next door to appear and to appear fast. To avoid just settling for anything, I need to foster clarity.

**"In the hallway," between opportunities when "one door closes, and you are waiting for the next door to open."**

Clarity, or the lack of it, shows up in many ways.

Phil, a recent college graduate, was clear about his desire to live abroad and contribute to society in a meaningful and productive manner. After several months of traveling, he landed in San Francisco. Phil took a part-time retail job that demanded he be available seven days a week from 10 AM to 10 PM. This did not match his vision for himself. Clear and committed to his goals, Phil fought off his frustration and disillusionment at his inability to quickly secure a position that would use his talents for the good of society. In spite of a very unpredictable work schedule and a less than ideal living situation, Phil stayed true to his values-based clarity of purpose. It served him well. He sought out and pursued opportunities that would use his talents. While the seven months it took him to secure an opportunity were definitely difficult for Phil, his dedication to his vision paid off handsomely. He was awarded a much-coveted position working in a third-world country using his talents to foster peace, cooperation, and understanding.

Lydia entered the workforce after her children were in school. Never having given much thought to her own career, she took various low-skill jobs. She only lasted several months before moving on. She just knew there must be a job she could love and would stay with it if only she could figure out what kind of work she wanted to do. Lydia's lack of clarity about her own talents and interests hindered her from making meaningful decisions about her career path. She struggled for nearly a year before she sought out career counseling. With the help of an excellent advisor, she was able to identify her strengths, interests, and talents and match them to job descriptions. Lydia used her newfound clarity to guide her in her job search, resulting in a position she not only loved, but that provided her with opportunities to further develop her career.

Matt, a senior operations director for a large automotive company lost his job his when company moved overseas. He spoke with great frustration about not knowing what his next position would be. We talked about the concept of being in the hallway and how it might be useful for him to focus on doing the things he loved while looking for a new position. He was able to keep his spirits up by adding going to the gym, volunteering at a homeless shelter, and undertaking some home projects he had been putting off. It certainly made being in the hallway a lot easier for him until he found a wonderful sales job in an entirely different industry.

**Knowing how to create your own clarity is not only possible, it's advisable.**

Creating clarity takes work. Knowing how to create your own clarity is not only possible, it's advisable. So, how can you create clarity? Most people want to get clear on where they are going and what they will be doing. People struggling with clarity often get stuck with the first question: "What do you want to do?" followed by the second question, "With whom do you want to do it?" When that happens, I start with the gifts they want to use.

## Gifts

**Your gifts include your talents, abilities, skills, interests, knowledge, attitudes, and experiences.**

Your gifts include your talents, abilities, skills, interests, knowledge, attitudes, and experiences. When you're clear about your gifts, you know which ones you want to experience, develop, and give. You are able to talk about them and know when you're using them—your choice. You know which ones are stronger than the others and which ones are your favorites. You know which ones are for giving and which ones aren't. You know which ones you would like to have, but don't. You can even create a game plan for developing more gifts. Remember: all gifts seek expression.

After retiring from a long career in management for a public utility, Marge downsized her large family home and moved into a lovely apartment. Her grown children were scattered around the country. Without the previous demands of her job, house, and children, she didn't know what to do. She was depressed and uninspired. A friend, wanting to help her come up with a plan, asked her to quickly name the three things she loved to do. Marge responded, "I love to sing, cook, and teach."

"Well, start with that," her friend suggested. Marge knew she couldn't teach singing. She could, however, rejoin a church choir she sang with years before her children left for college. And she had just talked with a friend who taught cooking in a program for low-income families that always needed teachers. It was enough clarity to get Marge started on a new life, leading to new and interesting people and experiences.

When you are unclear about your gifts, you have a hard time knowing exactly what it is you want to do with your life. You also experience difficulty in creating a life path in a manner that aims toward your Highest and Best. It's challenging to tell people what you want to do because, without clarity, there's no focus. You may want to be all things: "Jack of all Trades, Master of None." It's your default. You may find your life nice, but not great. You may be unsettled or bored and not know why.

**When you are unclear about your gifts, you have a hard time knowing exactly what it is you want to do with your life.**

You might be quite clear about your gifts and can rattle them off quickly. Or, you might need to think about them. If that's the case, try asking yourself:

- What are my three most memorable experiences in the past week, month, or year?
- What gifts or talents were I using?
- What gifts do I enjoy using while engaging in different aspects of my life?
- What do others see as my gifts?

Years ago while helping new coaches from around the world build their practices, I asked them what gifts they wanted to give. I discovered that many of them weren't exactly sure what their gifts were, let alone which ones they wanted to give. So, we began the process of exploration by talking about what they thought their gifts might be.

An insightful coach from Southern California introduced the idea of asking his family, friends, business associates, and acquaintances what they thought his gifts were. He made a list of their responses. He was pretty surprised with what he'd learned. For the next week he observed himself, identifying when he was using these gifts. He began to see himself in a whole new light. He was able to create clarity about his gifts and which ones he wanted to use in his coaching practice.

Don't be put off if those you ask to identify your gifts need a minute or two to think about your request. After all, it's not a common request.

Here is another exercise you might want to answer in your journal:

- Observe yourself while interacting with someone or engaged in an activity.
- If something feels particularly right or you like the results, make a note of it.
- What made it so good?
- What gifts, skills, or talents were you using?
- What were the other person's comments?
- What was happening inside of you?

**Rest assured, your own gifts are plentiful and diverse.**

As you gain clarity about your gifts, you can begin to quantify and define them. You know when you're using them and begin to call upon them as tools. Once you have a good handle on your list, you are ready to determine which ones are for giving. We all have gifts we want to keep private, saving them for those closest to us or just for ourselves. And then there are those gifts we just can't wait to share. It's important that you're clear on which ones are which.

**We all have gifts we want to keep private.**

Earlier, you made a diagram illustrating the gifts you brought to coaching. Using the same format, choose something you want clarity about. It can be about a relationship, career, retirement, anything for which you want to create a vision.

- Put the word defining what you are seeking clarity for in the middle.
- At the end of each spoke, list a gift you would like to use.
- Define each gift as much as possible.

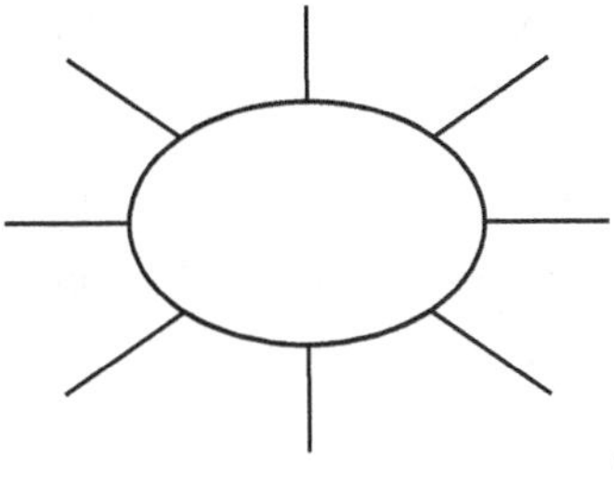

*Sample diagram*

Rest assured, your own gifts are plentiful and diverse. Some of them are tangible, others intangible. Again, they are your talents, abilities, skills, interests, knowledge, attitudes, and experiences. Highlight the gifts you would like to use. If you find that you are highlighting all of them, know that you have hit the jackpot. If, on the other hand, you would rather not use any of them, you might need to find another focus or dig around until you find ones you would like to use.

## Recipients

In addition to having clarity about the gifts you want to give, you also can decide with whom you would like to share your gifts. I am not talking about "shoulds," "coulds," or "makes sense to." These are someone else's ideas. Think about the qualities and attributes of the people you want to receive your gifts. Where might you find them? Your answers might include individuals, groups, or organizations.

Russell, a highly successful businessman from the entertainment industry, wanted to build a coaching practice but didn't appear to have the space for one. He seemed very busy, unable to put much energy into developing his practice. He was extremely clear about his gifts in business. I watched his body language and his facial expression as he discussed coaching business executives.

He looked uninspired. When I pointed this out to him, he was completely surprised. Russell had never considered the possibility that his practice wasn't growing because he didn't want to coach the people he had identified as obviously good candidates. As we explored other types of potential clients, he talked with great excitement about the possibility of coaching women business owners who were gutsy, creative, and making their mark in the world.

As Russell came to this realization, I could feel his heart opening up. I could hear it in his voice. His enthusiasm for coaching just exploded as he realized he had been chasing the wrong group of people. With this new insight, his practice became an exciting place for him to be. It didn't take long for him to start attracting his ideal clients with plenty of space to accommodate them.

Now it is your turn to identify the possible recipients of your gifts. Referring to your list of gifts:

- Make a list of who you would like to receive your gifts.
    - These can be individuals, groups, or organizations.
- Describe them in as much detail as possible.
- Explain why you want to give your gifts to these people in particular.

- Describe where you want to give your gifts. It might be a geographical location, a type of organizational setting, or within a particular group or function.

Your answers may make perfect sense or they may surprise you. It could have more to do with your love for a particular profession or industry, or maybe its gender, geographic location, culture, or type of person. Identify them by as many different descriptors as possible. Dig deep and create a clear picture. The more you know about them, the easier it will be for you to identify them.

With the clarity of knowing what you want to do and with whom you want to do it, you are in a much better position to seek and find opportunities that fulfill your dreams. With this clarity, you are now able to identify the steps to secure the right opportunities. Take the time for this important reflection.

**With the clarity of knowing what you want to do and with whom you want to do it, you are in a much better position to seek and find opportunities that fulfill your dreams.**

I encourage you to work on the issue of clarity. Unless you have a clear picture of your gifts, who you want to give them to, and what you want to do in your life, you will continue to walk around in a fog. Give yourself permission to work on this step. It can make the difference between a great life pursuing your Highest and Best, or a so-so one.

CHAPTER 8

# Space Requirements

*To live your life aiming for your Highest and Best,*
*you must have space for it.*

*People, work, play, and activities* all take varying degrees of space: time, physical, mental, emotional, and spiritual space. Manifesting your dreams and visions takes space. When you are clear about your space requirements and availability, you will be able to target and adjust your personal development to support your creations. As a coach, I always look at how well these spaces are tended as they have a direct impact on how well one creates their reality. You can do the same.

When you use your spaces well, things tend to go more smoothly and you have room in your life for what is important to you. When you understand the ebb and flow of your spaces, you have a better understanding of your life and how to navigate it as it changes. Your life expands and contracts in direct proportion to the amount of space available to you. These fluctuations make sense. You know what to do if you want to influence your spaces and you accept when you cannot.

**When you use your spaces well, things tend to go more smoothly and you have room in your life for what is important to you.**

When there is not enough space, you are cramped. Your ability to be present is compromised because you simply have no room in your life for what is important to you. You shove some of the most important things to the back of the line. Your efforts go unrewarded. You're frustrated. On the other hand, too much space creates its own set of problems.

Let's look at five space requirements I consider when I am coaching. These are basic to all of us: time, physical, mental, emotional, and spiritual. I also use them for my own self-reflection and evaluation. They can be guidelines for your conversations and observations of yourself and others.

Be gentle with yourself as you go through these requirements. You will most likely find you need to do some work on most if not all of these spaces. Be nice to yourself. Please don't take on too many at one time. No sense in overwhelming yourself. ...Baby steps will get you to your Highest and Best...a baseball bat won't!

**When there is not enough space, you are cramped.**

## Time

When you have time in your life for the things that are important to you, you feel fulfilled and satisfied. Your priorities are clear and aligned with your values. You have standards as to how you use your time and you have healthy boundaries that protect your standards. You know when to say yes; you know when to say no. You manage your time as a valuable asset. You have a good idea of how much time you need to accomplish tasks. You are realistic about what you can accomplish at different times in your life.

**When you have time in your life to do the things that are important to you, you feel fulfilled and satisfied. Your priorities are clear and aligned with your values.**

**When you don't have enough time or don't use your time well, you feel rushed and unfulfilled.**

When you don't have enough time or don't use your time well, you feel rushed and unfulfilled. You may do what you think you should do versus what you want to do. You may be unsure about what is important to you. Or, you're simply afraid to stand up for yourself. Your priorities may be confused. You may have no standards as to how you use your time, therefore, no boundaries. You may be wasting time, spending it foolishly. You are either unsure or unrealistic about how much time things take. You're late; you miss appointments, you forget.

When you have too much time, different problems can emerge.

Kelly entered college after having had an extremely busy high school career. During high school, she enjoyed a full academic life coupled with extracurricular activities in the performing arts and a part-time job at a local nursery. College, however, proved to be quite different for her. Unlike high school, her classes did not fill up her days. Performing arts opportunities at her school were limited to those majoring in the arts. Her father, whose own college career was marked by constantly scrambling for funds, insisted that he provide for her financially and that she should not have a job while in college. Her productivity and emotional health plummeted.

With so much free time on her hands, Kelly discovered that tasks she had accomplished quickly and easily in high school now took significantly longer. She learned the difficult but valuable lesson that time needed to accomplish tasks often expands and contracts according to the time available. It is called Parkinson's Law. After struggling for a semester, her father agreed that Kelly could add a volunteer job at a local school and more classes to her schedule. Her depression lifted and she regained the efficiency she had experienced in high school.

**At different stages in your life, you have different amounts of time.**

At different stages in your life, you have different amounts of time. Sometimes you have an enormous amount of time, space, and energy.

Sometimes you don't. Being realistic and flexible will enable you to move gracefully between your ever-changing time availability.

When our first son was born, I managed to keep my coaching practice at the level to which it had grown but cut back on public speaking. Fourteen months later, our second son was born and it was time to scale back even more. I let my client base shrink. As our kids got older, my time opened up and my client base increased to fill my new capacity.

The part that was so satisfying to me and the part I really want you to get is that these ideas work, often appearing to be magical. I leaned on my own tools. I was clear about my gifts and who I wanted to receive them. I honored my space requirements. Whenever I felt I had room, I simply acknowledged it. Believe it or not, new clients appeared. I was creating at my Highest and Best. It will happen for you as well.

Answer the following questions in your journal:

- What are the three to four most important things in my life?
- How much time have I given to what is important to me today or in the past week?
- What gets in my way from attending to what is important to me?
- Is my time limited because of other priorities?

- When don't I use my time well?
- Do I have too much time?
- Am I neglecting important areas of my life?
- Do I say yes when I should say no?
- Do I say no when I should say yes?
- How would I like to spend my time?

As you answer these questions, interesting observations and ideas may come to mind about the time you have and how you use it. You might find yourself wondering how to get a handle on your time.

Perhaps a review of how you're spending your time is in order. To get an overview, make a list of each activity you engage in for a couple of days. Note how much time you spend on each one. Be as complete as you can. For a more detailed accounting, you can create an hour-by-hour chart to fill in as you go. Review your entries to see how you are spending your time. It will also reveal any patterns you have developed. Compare your list or chart to what is important to you. Now you are in a better position to make appropriate changes to your schedule and habits.

To improve the way you use time, it may be helpful to block out certain times for specific activities and stick with it. Maybe you need a good time-management system that will help you keep your priorities in focus and assist you in determining how much time you need for the things that are important to you. This system could also help you schedule time for your priorities. Perhaps it's time to delegate or hire someone. You may discover that your current priorities don't leave much time for a particular activity or focus and your idea of a full life needs to be adjusted.

**Time is a precious commodity. Using it wisely will serve you well.**

Reviewing the time you have available and how you are using it is important to reaching your Highest and Best. Periodic reviews to help you determine if you need to make any adjustments can be a lifesaver. Time is a precious commodity. Using it wisely will serve you well.

## **Physical:** External

When your physical space supports you, you feel comfortable. You have the right amount of room and the right amount of things. You know where things are because everything has a home. It's as easy to find what you are looking for as it is for you to put it away. You have the right amount of workspace, lighting, and equipment. Everything is in good working order. You have the privacy you need without feeling isolated.

**When your physical space supports you, you feel comfortable.**

When you don't have enough physical space or it doesn't support you, it's harder to accomplish things. You feel cramped. Either you don't have enough space to spread out, you don't have the right tools, or your tools aren't in good working order. Your belongings don't have appropriate homes. You lose time when you can't find what you're looking for. Frustration is not a good companion for your Highest and Best.

**When you don't have enough physical space or it doesn't support you, it's harder to accomplish things.**

Have you ever seen a child's playroom where there are well-defined and labeled homes for all their toys, books, and art supplies? Their play is more productive and more creative. Their cleanup is quick, easy, and fun. This is in sharp contrast to children who play in disheveled spaces, their belongings strewn about. Their play is hampered, as is their creativity. The same thing is true for adults. If you want to take the joy out of cooking, make dinner in a messy kitchen!

One of the early questions I ask my clients is, "What does your desk look like right now?" Their response tells me a lot about their space, both mental and physical. Often, their first order of business is to create order in their office: clear off their desk and from that point on, keep it neat.

Bob, a construction engineer from Chicago, fiercely complained about his inability to finish projects. One look at his office filled with stacks, piles, and sticky notes explained it all. When I asked him how he developed the habit of creating such an office, he replied, "If I put anything away, I forget to do it." I asked him how that was working for him. He responded, "Well, obviously not too well because I'm not getting my projects done. I'm missing deadlines."

Bob needed help developing his focus, skills, attitudes, and habits to keep his desk and office orderly while staying on top of his projects. We created a system blending an easy filing system with time management and daily routines that would keep him on track. No longer would he need various piles covering his desk, floor, tables, and chairs. Bob developed an orderly method to put away and retrieve what he needed to accomplish his goals. He committed to a daily practice of using what he had learned. Once he got the hang of it, Bob was shocked at how productive he was.

Take a look at the physical spaces you live and work in.

- Are they working for me?
- Do I have what I need?
- Are things in good working order?
- Is there a place for everything?
- What habits do I have or need to develop to support my space?

When setting up my work and storage spaces, be it my office, kitchen, cupboards or closets, I imagine myself working in the space. I have even gone so far as to create a diagram of my space and labeled where I think things should go. This helps me determine what I need to make the most of each location. I make sure that the things I use regularly are stored close by and easy to reach. The items that are not routinely used are stored farther away, freeing up valuable work and storage space.

Take the action you need to create space for yourself that supports your Highest and Best and watch the changes that occur!

**Create space for yourself that supports your Highest and Best and watch the changes that occur!**

**Physical:** Internal

How you treat your body has a direct impact on the quality of your life. I am going to make this real simple…your body needs five basic things:

*Food*

- Do you make a point of eating mostly real food, seriously real food, as in the healthy kind: fresh, well-grown, kindly raised?

*Water*

- Are you drinking clean water and a lot of it—every day?

*Movement*

**How you treat your body has a direct impact on the quality of your life.**

- How do you love to move?
- Do you move often and with great enthusiasm?
- Do you engage in your favorite sport or exercise on a regular basis?

*Sleep*

- Are you getting good, quality sleep and enough of it?
- Are you sleeping too much?
    - This can cause its own problems or be an indication of other physical or emotional concerns.
- Do you know how much sleep you need to be your best?

*Air*

- We all breathe, but are you breathing deeply?
- When was the last time you consciously took a really deep, cleansing breath?
- Are you using your breath to keep you calm?
- How is the air quality in your living and work spaces?

For many of us, doing a good job supporting our physical bodies can be tough. Find what works for you and stick with it! Just don't give up. If you go astray, find your way back. When this happens to me—which of course it does—I pick food, water, or movement and focus on it for a couple of days. Soon, the second one comes looking for attention and the next thing I know, I am doing my best with all five areas and am much better off for it. Then I fall off and have to start over again. Sound familiar? You and I both know it is hard to get going, easier to keep going, and, at times, easy to fall off. We also know it is important not to give up. After all, how can we be our Highest and Best if we feel crummy from poor food choices, dehydration, lack of movement, not enough sleep, or shallow breathing? You can't, nor can I.

If you are on board with all of this and I am preaching to the choir, good for you. If you are not, I invite you to take a really good look at how you are treating your body. It truly affects your ability to live at your best.

When I addressed my food issues, I used the Focus, Skills, Attitudes, and Habits Method to guide me. I concluded that I didn't have the necessary culinary skills for my new focus. While I wished I could have bought those skills with a full-time cook, that wasn't feasible. Instead, I treated myself to a culinary school specializing in using foods for healing. Not only did I get the skills I needed, but it also transformed my attitude toward food as well as my habits. My only regret was that I didn't get these tools before raising our sons. Our meals would have been much healthier for all of us. You may not have space in your life for such an adventure. But I assure you, if you are motivated, you will be able to gain the skills you need to treat your body like royalty.

Here is what I encourage my clients (and you and me as well) to do:

- Evaluate yourself
  - Take a good look in the mirror.
    - How does my skin look?
    - How do my eyes look?
    - Am I at a good weight?
    - How is my muscle tone?
- Keeping a diary to track your food, water, movement, and/or sleep is a great way to get a clear picture of how you are treating yourself. Yes, it can be a pain in the neck to do, but you can get some excellent insight into yourself! You can find a variety of diaries online.
- Pick one thing to work on at a time, whichever one is easiest for you or the one you think will give you the biggest and fastest payoff.
- Spend some time learning about the one you pick.

- Create a plan and a way to hold yourself accountable.
- Once comfortable, add another one.
- If it would help, get support. Friends, family, or support groups are all possible options. We want you healthy!!!

It would be nice if our bodies would function at their best, independent of our decisions, but they don't.

Here are a few "baby steps" you might take:

- Take three deep breaths as you lay down to sleep at night and in the morning when you wake.
- Replace a dessert with your favorite fruit.
- Drink one more glass of water a day than you normally drink.
- Get out of the office or house and take a walk around the block.
- Go to bed 15 minutes earlier than usual or if you are sleeping too much, wake up 15 minutes earlier.

These small steps can make a big difference. Try one or two of these for a week and see what happens.

*Be nice to your body and it will be nice back!*

## Mental

Your mental space is filled with what you choose to think about, moment-to-moment, day-to-day. When you have adequate mental space, you have room to take on new ideas and think about things in detail. You have the space to learn and grow. You are mentally present in the moment. You think, hear, and respond unencumbered by concerns beyond your control. You are quick. You have easy access to your gifts. You bring your best to each day of your life.

**Your mental space is filled with what you choose to think about, moment-to-moment, day-to-day. When you have adequate mental space, you have room to take on new ideas and think about things in detail.**

When your mental space is cluttered, you have difficulty focusing. You drift from thought to thought. Your ability to be present is compromised. Your mental space may be cluttered simply with life's demands or what you're feeding your mind. Some call this "stinking thinking."

**When your mental space is cluttered, you have difficulty focusing.**

One of my favorite stories is about an Indian Chief who was describing the great battle between the good and evil wolves residing within every person. His son asked, "Which wolf will win?" The Chief responded, "Whichever one is fed."

Sonja found herself hooked on Facebook. John spent hours watching cable news. Stephen couldn't put down books about human atrocities. Nancy found that she became the go-to person for everyone else's problems. Each of them found their mental space being taken up by ideas, people, and images that were not supporting them at their Highest and Best. When they committed to filling their minds with more positive, productive ideas, activities and people, their mental space opened for more fulfilling thoughts and fulfillment each day.

As a child, your thoughts, beliefs, and behaviors were influenced and molded by your family, school, and community. Your childhood influences impact how you think and how you see the world today. It is your choice as well as your opportunity to change anything that does not support who you want to be today. If it does not serve your Highest and Best, you can change the dynamic to make it match your vision of your Highest and Best.

**Your childhood influences impact how you think and how you see the world today.**

To create mental space, begin by looking at what you are feeding your mind.

Take a minute and note:

- What do I find myself drawn to?
- Am I feeding my mind good, healthy, life-giving thoughts, or harsh images, worry, and discontent?

- Do I need to put myself on a "news" diet?
- Do I need to limit the time I spend with certain people?
- What might be bugging me:
  - unfinished projects
  - repairs
  - making do
  - relationship(s) that don't work for me
  - unresolved issues of my past
  - making necessary plans for an upcoming event or project
- What thoughts and ideas did I bring from my childhood that might be hurting me now?

Whatever grabs your mind and takes you off your focus should be handled. Doing so will clear up important mental as well as emotional space. Keeping your mind fresh and open is an invitation for new and interesting things.

Another way to create mental space is through mind-clearing activities such as early morning walks, prayer, meditation, reading inspirational messages, listening to calming music, or physical exercise. Believe it or not, even clearing up clutter will have a positive effect on your mental space.

**Keeping your mind fresh and open is an invitation for new and interesting things.**

My favorite mind-clearing activity is deep breathing. To me, it is invaluable because I can call on it at any moment, under any circumstances. I breathe in good thoughts, making positive affirmations with each inhale. As I exhale, I imagine all the negative thoughts and feelings I am harboring come rushing out.

I encourage you to spend some quiet time by yourself every day. Without the distraction of other people or the media, you can clear your mind and your thoughts. I guarantee you, with practice, you will come to protect your precious alone-time and see it as vital to your well-being. In fact, as you improve your ability to keep your mind clear, you will have more mental space available for your Highest and Best creations.

### Emotional

Healthy emotional space gives you room to fully experience a whole range of emotions without fear or reservation. You understand the emotions you are experiencing and are confident in your ability to be present with them. You are mindful of their messages and capable of heeding their advice. You can be present with others in their emotional space. Aware of others' feelings, you have no need or desire to feel their feelings for them or to stop them from feeling

**Healthy emotional space gives you room to fully experience a whole range of emotions without fear or reservation.**

them for themselves. You understand the language of emotion and help when a translation is needed.

Unhealthy emotional space makes experiencing emotions difficult. It can show up as anxiety, depression, chaotic thinking, loss of appetite, loss of motivation or addictions. It affects our daily life, our relationships, our work, and our success. Resolving unhealthy emotional states may require the help of a professional such as a therapist or psychiatrist. It's difficult to coach someone whose emotional space is unhealthy.

**Unhealthy emotional space ... affects our daily life, our relationships, our work, and our success.**

In every life, there are times when emotional space becomes limited by an event. They are often identified by the stress test—birth of a child, the death of a loved one, moving, loss of a job, divorce, even vacations. When you are accustomed to having plenty of emotional space, you often move through these times knowing that it is limited in duration as well as intensity. Sometimes the stress takes up all of your emotional space. When you don't have enough space, you run the risk of getting stuck and often need help getting unstuck.

After a divorce that was a long time in the making, William found that his emotional state was limited. He could not be present with himself, his work, his children, or his friends. He lost his clarity and his focus. He began engaging in activities and substances that took him away from his Highest and Best to his lowest and worst.

Wisely, William sought out the support of an excellent therapist. Within time, he realized he was trying to distract himself rather than deal with the emotional fallout that came with his divorce. He became clear that the clutter of his past was keeping him from the life he wanted. He resolved childhood issues, saw his part in the destruction of his marriage, and began to live his life in a manner that was truly aimed at his Highest and Best.

We all have, to varying degrees, emotional clutter. Past unresolved issues, grudges, judgments, blocks, resistance — all taking up space; space that could be better used for the present. Like the piles on your desk, clutter is clutter. It's best to clear it away. Again, if you can deal with the clutter by yourself, by all means, do so. There are definitely excellent skills that you may or may not have that can get the job done. If you find yourself unable to clear away the emotional clutter, find professional help. It is available in books, online, and with friends, family, clergy, counselors, and therapists.

You may need emotional help if you:

- feel like you need help, you probably do
- find yourself worrying excessively

- have prolonged periods of being blue
- have emotional outbursts
- have trouble sleeping
- have difficulty in your relationships
- find yourself sabotaging your efforts
- are anxious or depressed
- keep losing things like jobs, friends, opportunities
- use drugs, alcohol, or activities to escape

If you discover that someone you are helping or coaching is emotionally unhealthy, help them find the right help. If you are emotionally unhealthy, please do find help! There's no need for suffering. People who are in emotional pain often hurt other people without realizing it. Please keep in mind: asking someone to help you move furniture doesn't mean you are physically disabled just as seeking emotional help does not mean you are crazy, disturbed, or pathological. What is important is that you get the support you need to be your best.

Being happy and emotionally healthy is a goal we all want to achieve and maintain. However, we don't just get there overnight. Sometimes we need to work at it. Sometimes we need to allow others to work with us so we can move to our

**Being happy and emotionally healthy is a goal we all want to achieve and maintain.**

Highest and Best. None of us get to be happy all the time. We do, however, need to know how to find our way back to a happy, healthy state of mind. It is essential for living at your Highest and Best.

## Spiritual

Your spiritual space is defined by your beliefs and a relationship with that which is greater than you. There are many names, beliefs, and paths leading to and enhancing your spiritual space. When your spiritual space is open, your guidance and gifts are magnificent. You are better able to access your gifts and you live your life in the flow. You move through your days with grace and peace. You experience understanding and patience.

**Your spiritual space is defined by your beliefs and a relationship with that which is greater than you.**

When your spiritual space is cluttered or blocked, you have difficulty accessing your intuition, your clarity, and your higher self or higher power. You become easily frustrated, out of sync; you lose your flow. You are denied the most valuable resource of all: that still, small voice within which comes from something far greater than yourself.

Jennifer, an experienced and dedicated classroom teacher, began having trouble dealing with a couple of disruptive students. She was surprised and dismayed when her responses led to more misbehavior from her students. In the past, these types of problems had been easy for her to handle.

Her principal, noticing that Jennifer had become increasingly unable to cope with disruptive students, asked her point blank, "This didn't use to be a problem. What did you do before when your students misbehaved?" She surprised herself and her principal by her immediate response. "Oh, I just asked God to speak to them through me and they always listened." For reasons Jennifer couldn't explain, she had stopped using her very powerful connection.

There are many ways to open and expand your spiritual channels. Prayer, meditation, spiritual writings, listening to music, or attending religious services are some of the most common. You may have a daily spiritual habit or turn to these as needed. Coaches often say a prayer or ask their higher power for guidance before coaching sessions. You would be amazed at the guidance you can receive in the moment…any moment, simply by asking.

**There are many ways to open and expand your spiritual channels.**

Tending to your connection and the flow of guidance and information is incredibly important to create your life at its Highest and Best. You may want to answer the following questions:

- What is my spiritual connection?
- Is it strong or weak?
- How well am I tending to my spiritual space?
- How often do I turn to my spiritual connection for guidance?

- Do I have a well-defined spiritual practice or habit?
- Do I need to recommit to a spiritual practice, deepen an existing one, or begin a new one?

Over the next week, try asking for guidance from your higher power on matters large and small. It might be a difficult conversation, or a decision you need to make. I can't tell you how many times I have received the words to give comfort, advice, or respond to ideas that are contrary to my very core beliefs. I am always amazed. You may also find that you are guided to seek out clergy or attend religious services. You might even be guided to take a walk. As you nurture your spiritual relationship, you will nurture yourself and your Highest and Best.

This list of space requirements is by no means exhaustive nor the discussion complete. You may discover that some of the space requirements make more sense to you than others. You may also find other areas to include. The important thing to remember is this: to live your life aiming for your Highest and Best, you must have space for it. The larger and more complicated your life, the more significant your space requirements. It is true for you and those you coach. Remember, you are not looking for perfection, only improvement!

**To live your life aiming for your Highest and Best, you must have space for it.**

CHAPTER 9

# Personal Development

*Putting you on the fast track to your Highest and Best*

*Your personal development* contributes to your ability to create a full and fulfilling life at your Highest and Best. It occurs within the context of your spaces, your gifts, and your relationships. It may be within your personal, professional, spiritual, family, or community life. It generally involves your focus, skills, attitudes, and habits.

When you are developing, you are learning and growing. You know who you are, who you are becoming, and what you want to do. You are open to new ideas, concepts, and change. You understand that there is so much more to learn and you are literally at the tip of your own iceberg. You experience life with eyes of wonderment and excitement. New opportunities appear; paths open that previously had been closed. Your coaching ability and coachability are high and your awareness is growing.

When you're not developing, you're stuck. You cling to old ideas, unable to see possibilities. You have no room for ideas and opinions that don't support the ones you already hold. You think you know all the answers. Life becomes dull, predictable. You believe that who you are is who you are and there's not a lot you can do about it. You may be stuck without even realizing it, ruining relationships along the way.

Julie and Frank were discussing politics. Frank makes a statement that doesn't confirm Julie's beliefs and opinions. Julie gets boiling mad and makes a quick exit. Frank has had the same experience with Julie when discussing any number of other topics. Frank realized that Julie's inability to consider ideas and opinions that conflict with her tightly held ideas and beliefs makes it impossible for them to discuss most topics in a meaningful way. Julie had no respect or room for Frank's opinions. Soon, Frank had no respect for Julie's opinion. The hope of ever finding any common ground goes out the window. Their friendship suffers. This is definitely not leading them to their Highest and Best.

There is a great deal of this "shutting down" going on in our world today. The ideas and tools presented in *Simply Coaching* can be a helpful guide in keeping your conversations open and positive while striving to understand the other person. And if both people are using it, you both might learn something, opening yourself up to new ideas and growth. You may even find that you have more to agree on than you had previously thought.

There is a great deal of this "shutting down" going on in our world today.

Personal development requires a desire to learn and grow. It requires focus and an open mind. With infinite ways to develop, look for opportunities in your everyday life. Personal or professional relationships and challenges, an area of interest, community involvement, political opportunities, and spiritual quests are ripe with opportunities for lessons and growth. Online or in-person classes may be the best way for you to learn. Or you might prefer hands-on experiences, a coach, an on-the-job training program, or college. It doesn't matter. It's your life, your learning.

Be on the lookout for specific clues. As a coach, I have always been amazed at the number of times my clients present needs that mirror my own. I have often said that my clients reflect what I need to learn, need to reinforce, or need to review. I can't tell you how often I focused a client on time-management when I needed to do the same. You can only imagine the mirror I have had as I wrote this book! With that in mind, you might ask yourself what you see in your world that may provide insights into your own need for personal development.

Personal development requires a desire to learn and grow.

Personal development puts you on the fast track, growing and learning fascinating things about yourself, others, and the world around you. As I said earlier, it can be very useful to use the concepts of clarity, space, and development as a guide to create your own "State of the Me" report. From there, you can focus on a couple of specific things. Where you focus and what you choose to do next are up to you. Take your time. Don't try to tackle them all at once. No sense in overwhelming yourself. That would not be in your best interest, now would it?

**Personal development puts you on the fast track, growing and learning fascinating things about yourself, others, and the world around you.**

As you work on being your Highest and Best, keep in mind that how you see yourself will change as you allow yourself to grow and mature into the amazing person you were created to be. Time will become more kind to you as you give yourself permission to be your best. You will find that time will expand to accomplish your dreams. I promise: many doors will open to you as you become who you were created to be at your Highest and Best!

**Use the concepts of clarity, space, and development as a guide to create your own "State of Me" report.**

# Afterword

*Like it or not, this is your life!* It is your creation to cultivate or to waste. The decision is yours. Regardless of your circumstances, your ancestry, your past decisions, good or bad, it is your life and your responsibility. How you choose to live your life affects both your internal and external experiences. Your choices also impact those you are closest to as well as others in society, near and far. What choices will you make today that will guide you to your Highest and Best self?

When I said we would like you to be your Highest and Best, I meant it. I don't care which words you relate to on the cover of this book or if your circumstances are ideal or not, or how bad you have had it—it doesn't matter; we need you to be your best! We need me to be my best. We need the gal and guy next door to be their best. We must want it for everyone. With this mindset, we will all be on the fast track to a much better world for you and everyone else!

"But where do I begin?" you might well ask.

"Fundamentals," I reply. "Let's focus on the fundamentals of dreams and reality, with all the 'This is easy!' 'What were you thinking?' 'Seriously, you really think I can do all this?' and, 'Wow, that is an interesting way to look at myself!' moments that will follow."

*Simply Coaching* has given you these fundamentals. It has provided you with tools and ideas to support you in your quest to be better tomorrow than you are today. Explore them, apply them to your life, and watch what happens.

As I am so fond of saying, it is in our best interest for each of us to aim for our Highest and Best each moment of each and every day, and to respect and encourage others to do the same. It takes courage to be true to yourself and your values. Some days will look great and others not so…it this the nature of life. The important thing is for each of us to strive to be our best. Ultimately, it is up to you to choose how you direct your life and interact with others. Please choose well.

Be gentle with yourself as you incorporate these ideas into your daily life. Remember, Baby Steps!

Here's to you! With grace and dignity, you will achieve your Highest and Best!

Here's to your
Highest and Best!

# In Gratitude

My Higher Power for using me as a vessel for the ideas presented in *Simply Coaching*—then and now.

Skip Borst, the first coach to have championed my work and ensured the ideas in *Simply Coaching* (1997) found their way into the rules and regulations of the coaching industry.

Pat Williams for giving Simply Coaching wings to travel around the world, and an insightful preface for this new *Simply Coaching*.

The early adopters of *Simply Coaching*, making it their own in their practices, training programs and books.

My students and clients, there are no better teachers.

Those whose stories grace the ideas within, your experiences and journeys benefit so many.

The professionals who have helped me throughout the years: teachers, healers, therapists, artists, editors, and coaches—all with grace, dignity, and integrity.

My family and friends, you make life fascinating, exciting and worthwhile.

John Coffey, your support means the world to me.

My beloved sons, Christopher and Michael Coffey, you are my greatest gifts and inspiration.

And You. Thank you, thank you, thank you for championing the Highest and Best in yourself and others!

# About Lynn

*Ever the maverick,* and standard holder, Lynn always looks for ways to make the world a little bit better. Her childhood "Smile Route" taught her the value of looking into someone's eyes with joy and acceptance. The impact of her original *Simply Coaching* taught her the importance of sharing her gifts. A favorite teacher among children and adults and a successful businesswoman, entrepreneur and business coach, Lynn received a BS in Education from the University of Cincinnati, and an MBA from Pepperdine University. She was an early recipient of the designation of Master Certified Coach, MCC. A resident of Denver, Colorado, Lynn is happy to be out in the world once again, sharing what she knows.

Lynn welcomes opportunities to speak with young, old, and in-between, near and far, individually and in groups as a speaker, lecturer, and friend. Please contact her at *Lynn@SimplyCoaching.com.*

# Index


Accountability, 18–19, 50, 138

Addiction, 78, 143

Alcohol, 47, 145

Anxiety, 37, 78, 143

**Attitudes,** 24, 40–41, 49, 86
- Changing, 42
- Effects of, 43–44, 86, 87
- Journal Questions, 45
- Unhealthy, 87

Becoming a Professional Coach, vii

Big Picture/Detail, 23, 25, **30–33,** 81–82

Borst, Skip, 156

**Boundaries,** 6, 8, 11, **91–109,** 127
- Coaching, 106-107
- Diagram, 93-94
- External, 94–95
- Feedback, 93
- Healthy, 93
- Internal, 94–95
- Intentional, 92
- Journal Questions, 107
- Personal 92, 93–94, 96, 101, 102, 103, 104, 106–107
- Protecting, 93
- Self-boundaries, 94-100
- Working knowledge, 11
- Internal and External, 94–95

**Clarity,** 5, 8, 11, 54, 64, 66, 77, 109, 110, 113–114, 124, 152
- Coaching, 77, 113
- Conversation, 53
- Creating, 117, 120
- Concept of, 113, 152
- Gaining 64, 66, 103, 121, 143
- Gifts of, 110, 117
- Journal Questions, 119
- Lack of, 114–116, 119, 146
- Listening for, 54

**Coaching,** 11, 21, 27, 29, 38, 39, 63, 64, 70, 74, 81, 86, 88, 90, 110, 121, 123, 126, 147
Ability, 8, 49 149
Career, 67, 68
Cautions, 8
Clarity Conversations 4, 10, 53-54, 79, 109, 111
Emotional stability and, 145
Industry, 1, 6, 156
Models, 23
Moment, 5
Name of, 6
Practice, 109, 120, 122
Principles, 2
Process, 57, 61
Professional, 75, 113
Purpose, 1, 3, 77, 78, 129
Relationships, 15
Results, 4
Role, 73,
Self, 82, 84
Skills, 4, 10
Standards and Boundaries, for, 106
Styles, 6–7
Tools, 10, 51

**Conversations,** vii, 10, **53–80,** 150
Meaningful 3-5, 8, 61
Coaching, 24, 29

Core Competencies Coaching Profession, vi, 1, 156

Depression (depressed) 118, 128, 143, 145

**Development**
Coaching, v, 1
Personal, 4, 8, 11, 45, 49, 109–111, 125, 149–152

Drugs, 145

**Emotional**
Clutter, 14, 143
Health, 128, 142–145
Help, 30, 143 -145
Space, 11, 125–126, 141, **142–146**

Entrepreneurial Field of Rabbits, 28–29

**Floodlight,** 54–55, **74–77,** 78, 83, 85, 87, 89

**Focus,** 10, 23–24, **25–34,** 110, 111
Big Picture/Detail, 30–33, 81–82
Chaotic, 26–27
Coaching, 23–24, 81–84
Defined, 25
Focus, 33

Highest and Best, 14, 16, 18
Journal Questions, 18–19
Moving, 27–29
Positive, 62
Tools, 4
Wrong, 29–30

**Gifts,** 4–7, 42, 110, 113–114, **117–124**
Accessing, 139, 146
Coaching, 119–120
Highest and Best, 149
Journal Questions, 120–121
Sharing, 122–124, 155

**Goals,** 18–19, 21, 25, 28, 33, 34, 87, 88, 115, 133
Focus, 33
Skills, 34-35

**Habits,** 27, 45, **45–48,** 130
Bad, 45–46
Changing, 47–48, 88–89
Counterproductive, 46
Creating new, 47–48
Defined, 45
Good, 24, 45, 88
Journal Questions, 48

**Highest and Best,** 3, 4, 5, 9, **13–22,** 45, 53, 55, 67, 77, 78, 79, 80, 132, 134, 136, 140, 144, 146, 147, 148,153–154
Mindset, 13–14, 153–154

Inner Voice, 57, 60–61, 76 149,

Institute for Life Coach Training, vi

Interaction, 2–3

International Coach Federation, vi

**Journaling**
Attitudes, 45
Boundaries, 107
Clarity, 117
Focus, 33
Emotional Space, 144-145
Focus, 33
Gifts, 65, 79, 107, 120, 129–130
Goals, 18, 19, 40
Habits, 48
Highest and Best 18
Listening, Mirror Path Floodlight, 79
Mental Space, 140-141
Physical Space, 133, 134-135, 137-138

**Journaling** (contuned)
Skills, 40
Spiritual Space, 147-148
Standards and Boundaries, 104, 106, 107
Time, 129-130

**Listen, Mirror, Path, Floodlight Method of Coaching,** 10, **53- 80,** 81

**Listening, 56–57,** 82
Inner and inside 57, 58, 59, 60–61, 70, 76, 79

**Mental**
Habits, 88
Health continuum, 77–78
Health professionals 87, 89, 109
Space, 110, **139–142**

Mind-clearing, 141–142

**Mirroring,** 54–55, **61–68,** 69, 70, 71, 82, 84, 86, 88, 110, 151
Coaching, 82, 84, 86, 88, 111
State of the Me Report, 110

Parkinson's Law, 128

**Path, 68–69,** 70–72, 73–74, 83, 85, 87, 88

**Permission,** 21-22
Succeed, 21- 22
Quit, 21

**Personal**
Accountability, 18–19
Boundaries, 93–94, 96, 101, 102, 103, 104, 106–107
Gifts, 117–119, 120, 121–122
Insight, 2, 8
Interactions 2–3
Personal Space, 110, 125
Power, 4
Relationships, 78
Roles, 6
Skills, 4–6
Space, 110, 125
Standards, 91, 105
Time, 127, 129–131

**Personal Development,** 11, 111, 125, **149–152**

Personality Disorders, 78

**Physical**
External, 131-134
Internal, 134-138
Journal Questions,144-145

Selves, 45, 88
Space, 131-139
Well-being, 134–136, 137–138

**Powerful Four Method of Coaching,** 10, **23–51,** 49, 51, 81, 90

**Questions,** 56, 57, 60, 61, 65, 81, 82, 132
meaningful, 7

Quitting, 21

**Relationships,** 14, 15, 22, 121, 141, 143,145,149, 150, 151
Abusive, 21, 102
Coaching, 15, 77, 78
Interpersonal, 15, 44
Personal, 78
Satisfying, 9, 12,
Spiritual, 146,148

Sabotaging, 46, 88, 154

**Skills,** 8, 9, 24, 27, **34–40,** 84, 85,
122, 133, 136, 137, 144, 139
Acquiring, 39–40, 72, 136
Coaching, 3, 6, 84-85
Communications, 2
Defined, 84
Gifts, 117, 120
Missing, 33, 35–37, 44, 49, 50, 136
Unattainable, 39

***Simply Coaching, Ideas, Strategies, Methodologies and Philosophies About Coaching For Coaches,*** ii

State of the Me Report, 110

**Spiritual,** 91, 151
Connection, 67, 146, 147–148
Guide, 6
Practice, 148
Relationships, 146, 148
Space, 11, 110, 125, 126, **146–148,** 149

**Standards,** 8, 11, **91–94,** 95, 97, 98, 102, 106, 109
Coaching, 1, 6
Defined, 191-192
Double, 101
High, 100
Personal, 91–92, 94, 96, 100–101, 102, 103, 104, 106–107
Time, 127

**Standards and Boundaries,**
6, 8, 9, **91–108,** 106–107, 109
Clear, 92, 103
Coaching, 106-107
Identifying, 92
Rigid, 104
Weak, 104
Invisible, 103
Personal, 92
Support, 93
Time, 127

**Styles,**
Coaching, vii, 6, 7, 53, 63
Personality, 46

**Time,** 127–130
Being on, 95–96
Loosing, 132
Management, 27, 33, 49, 76, 130–131, 133
Quiet, 142
Restraints, 127, 129–131, 131–132, 133
Space, 11, 110, 125, 126
Too much, 128

Williams, Patrick vi-vii, 156

professor • leader • mother • nurse • graduate • volunteer • minister •
artist • gofer • geologist • advocate • business owner • farmer • author •
teacher • uncle • intern • coach • follower • chef • patriarch •

judge • elder • manager • cousin • counselor • doctor • pastor • grandmother • psychiatrist • refugee
musician • father • cleric • stage manager • caregiver • tailor • actor • parent • mathematician
chaplain • student • psychic • president • paramedic • aunt • cantor • architect • florist

coach • warden • inspector • rabbi • financier • brother • psychologist • handyman • custodian
ceo • conductor • scientist • bishop • comedian • cashier • journalist • dancer • techie

# Pass Along Copy

You may have received this book from someone who cares about you and thought you might find it worthwhile. Please take what works for you, leave what doesn't, then pass it along.

3-12-2020 *To Your Highest and Best!* Tallahassee Fla

Pass Along Copy Initiated by: Lynn Coffey

Pass Along to: Little Library

Pass Along to: ______________________

Pass Along to: ______________________

Pass Along to: ______________________

Pass Along to: ______________________

Pass Along to: ______________________

Pass Along to: ______________________

Pass Along to: ______________________

Pass Along to: ______________________

Pass Along to: ______________________

*If you would prefer your own print copy or*
*to receive this material in eBook or audio format,*
*please go to* **SimplyCoaching.com**.

futurist • grandfather • masseuse • politician • phlebotomist •
child • principal • police officer • agent • sister • adult • teacher •
mentor • teenager • administrator • miner • lawyer • social worker •

CPSIA information can be obtained
at www.ICGtesting.com
Printed in the USA
FSHW021345191219

9 780999 819906